T0301318

Ethics and Uncertainty

For Edwina, Logan, and Jeremy

Ethics and Uncertainty

The Economics of John M. Keynes and Frank H. Knight

William B. Greer

Chair, Area of Professional Learning and J. Henry Kegley
Associate Professor of Business and Economics
Milligan College, Tennessee, USA

Edward Elgar
Cheltenham, UK • Northampton, MA, USA

© William B. Greer 2000

All rights reserved. No part of this publication may be reproduced, stored in a
retrieval system or transmitted in any form or by any means, electronic,
mechanical or photocopying, recording, or otherwise without the prior
permission of the publisher.

Published by
Edward Elgar Publishing Limited
Glensanda House
Montpellier Parade
Cheltenham
Glos GL50 1UA
UK

Edward Elgar Publishing, Inc.
136 West Street
Suite 202
Northampton
Massachusetts 01060
USA

This book has been printed on demand to keep the title in print.

A catalogue record for this book
is available from the British Library

Library of Congress Cataloguing in Publication Data
Greer, William B., 1962–
    Ethics and uncertainty : the economics of John M. Keynes and Frank H.
Knight / William B. Greer.
      p. cm.
Includes bibliographical references and index.
    1. Economics—Moral and ethical aspects. 2. Economic policy—Moral
and ethical aspects. 3. Economic development—Moral and ethical aspects.
4. Keynes, John Maynard, 1883–1946 5. Knight, Frank Hyneman, 1885–
I. Title.

HB72.G736 2000
330.15'6—dc21   00–034833

ISBN 1 84064 445 1

Contents

Preface

In this pathbreaking work, Bill Greer has provided a masterful exposition explaining why John Maynard Keynes and Frank Hyneman Knight shared the same criticism of classical theory in terms of decision making under 'uncertainty', yet apparently reached different views of the value of unfettered markets for goods and labor. The focus of Greer's study is why these two great geniuses who placed the concept of uncertainty clearly at the center of their economic theory came to radically different policies.

The theological and conservative upbringing of Frank Knight is contrasted with Maynard Keynes' liberal, urbane background. Greer then explains how these differences in background during their formative years affected the two men's thinking and their theories regarding uncertainty and the economic process. Nevertheless, despite these differences of upbringing, temperament and opinion, both Knight and Keynes remained passionate in their concern for the ultimate welfare and improvement of mankind.

Both Knight and Keynes recognized the potential conflict between decisions taken in one's own self interest and actions taken for the good of a civil society. Greer points out that it is this distinction between the interests of the individual and society that brings about the concern for the ethics of economics which motivated Keynes and Knight. Both men exhibited an ethical and moral concern regarding truth, liberty, and the freedom of the individual to pursue goals that were not constrained by the unnecessary idleness of economic resources that often occurred in *laissez-faire* market systems.

Greer shows how family background, religious upbringing, education, and exposure to certain intellectual influences caused Knight to argue that uncertainty was best dealt with via free markets with little political involvement on the part of the state. Significant differences in the background of Keynes, on the other hand, led him to believe that freedom and efficiency could be provided by free markets only after the State exercised some central controls over aggregate demand to assure full employment. Greer explains why these men had such different attitudes and how it affected their economic analysis.

Unlike some modern economic practitioners, both Keynes and Knight were concerned with ethics. Each hoped to find the way that economic analysis could be used for the betterment of society. Greer demonstrates how the influences of background, religion, and rural simplicity versus urbane sophistication account for the apparent paradox that lead Knight and Keynes to contrasting views of reality. Knight remained the skeptic and maintained cynical views of reality throughout his life, while Keynes remained the perpetual optimist who fervently believed that prudent statesmanship could manage human nature to provide a civil society where all benefited. Finally, Greer analyzes the contrasts in each man's philosophy and outlooks for the future, as well as their views on a 'middle way' for society to solve its economic problems.

Greer concludes that, as we enter the new millennium, there remains the challenge of developing a global economic system where all members of society benefit while the individual freedoms of an orderly free-market system are preserved. Greer's discussion will convince the fair-minded reader that the development of such a civilized economic system requires a focus on the ethical ramifications of decision making under uncertainty. This, however, as Greer concludes 'requires an understanding of human behavior that extends beyond the realm of calculus and into the realm of ethics and philosophy, ground that many economists fear to tread'.

Paul Davidson
Holly Chair of Excellence,
University of Tennessee

Introduction

As this introduction is being written, civilization has just celebrated its entry into the twenty-first century. With much fanfare and enthusiasm, the calendars of the world have turned the page, ushering in not only a new century, but also a new millennium. Except, of course, to those who suggested that the celebration was premature, with the year 2000 actually being the *last* year of the twentieth century and the second millennium, rather than the beginning of the next. However, the anticipated arrival of the year 2000 could not be characterized as one of unanimous positive excitement, even for those celebrating the turn of the millennium. Rather, the year 1999 was marked with a decided apprehension and uncertainty regarding the effect of entry into the twenty-first century. As the year came to a close, an increasing number of individuals began to wonder what effect this historic step in time would have upon mankind and the complex environment mankind has created.

Earlier centuries have passed before and many millennia have come and gone, all without critical disruption to the structures and institutions that make up the fabric of society. The end of the twentieth century is, however, unlike the end of any century before. Specifically, mankind's dependence upon the trappings of the electronic age, especially advanced communication systems and computer technology, has left him feeling more vulnerable and at the mercy of his own creations. The fear that the dreaded 'Y2K bug' might rear its head at the stroke of midnight on January 1, 2000 brought with it an unprecedented level of anxiety and uncertainty. The result was the widespread stockpiling of non-perishable food, bottled water, and the hoarding of cash, against the possibility of some catastrophic worldwide computer failure. To be sure, not everyone acted as though some great apocalypse was at hand, but there were many people who did.

Perhaps it is under these sorts of conditions that the uncertainty of the future becomes so evident, even to those who have for so long suggested that uncertainty poses no real problem for society, as long as the tools of probability analysis are at our disposal to extend statistically the history of the past into the future. While an event like the coming of a new millennium may in itself be of such a unique and unpredictable nature that the tools of statistics might not apply, society must nonetheless deal with such true uncertainty in one form or another on a regular basis. While fear of the Y2K bug may have resulted in an exaggerated response to the uncertainty of the future, it nonetheless represents a microcosm of what has forever been the reaction of people when faced with the unknown. Unfortunately, the vast majority of economists have often failed to recognize the prevalence and impact of such uncertainty upon human behavior.

Rather than accept the reality that human behavior may exhibit a degree of irrationality when faced with uncertainty, economists have often ignored such a possibility, preferring to cling to the assumption that rational, utility-maximizing individuals are always able to deal with uncertainty by holding an unwavering faith in the statistical predictability of the future. Such a belief has led many economists to perpetuate the notion that economic agents function best within a free-market economy and that the result will be full employment, stable prices, and general economic well-being for all. The twentieth century, despite closing with a generally healthy economy in place worldwide, was nonetheless a period marked by increasingly severe business cycles, especially during the first half of the century.

If the tenets of classical economic theory were to hold true, the economy would be free of such turbulence as the severe involuntary unemployment that marked the 1930s in America and elsewhere. There were two economists, however, who questioned the previously accepted axioms of classical economic theory and viewed uncertainty in a critical and important new way. While both maintained different views regarding the role and purpose of economic theory and the degree to which external influence should be exerted upon an economic system, they both nonetheless incorporated uncertainty in their economic analysis as few have done before or since.

John Maynard Keynes built his *General Theory* upon the assumption of an entrepreneurial economy in which money matters because of the existence of uncertainty. Frank Hyneman Knight recognized the existence of uncertainty when he distinguished it from risk, incorporating each into his articulation of the classical economic model. Moreover, both economists concerned themselves with the ethical implications of decision making in the face of such uncertainty. In so doing, Keynes and Knight are as much philosophers as economists.

This book examines the ethical dimension of uncertainty within the economic theories of Knight and Keynes. Intellectual and theological influences upon their respective theories of probability and uncertainty are considered. The role of uncertainty in defining the purpose and method of economics and leading to their divergent economic outlooks and policy recommendations is also investigated.

The results of this investigation indicate that, despite their common emphasis, both Knight and Keynes viewed the role of uncertainty from different perspectives, derived from significant, formative influences upon their thinking and differing views regarding the role and purpose of economic theory as applied to the real world. The intellectualism into which Keynes was born was based upon logic, science, and rational thinking. The resulting enlightened thinking led Keynes to consider individual and collective action positively, enabling society to take purposeful, deliberate action, in the face of an uncertain, non-ergodic future.

The theological, conservative thinking from which Knight emerged left him cynical and critical of the established orthodoxy. While accepting its theoretical basis, Knight criticized classical theory for omitting uncertainty as an endogenous variable and for the assumed rationality of economic man. Knight's pessimism led him to suggest the government assume a negative role, limited to establishing and enforcing 'rules of the game' to ensure the smooth operation of a system of otherwise free markets.

Nevertheless, both economists recognized the dramatic impact of uncertainty upon individual and collective decision making. Their mutual abhorrence for the inevitable results of unrestrained capitalism led each to suggest that economics be used to improve the conditions of society. Both Knight and Keynes remained passionate in their concern for the ultimate welfare and improvement of mankind, despite differences of opinion as to how this goal is to be achieved. The goal of economists today, as time marches onward through the new millennium, should be to follow the lead of Knight and Keynes, and base contemporary economic policy formulation upon the inclusion of uncertainty as an endogenous variable, one that must be considered when dealing with the often irrational economic agents living within a non-ergodic world.

This book is the result of my doctoral dissertation research, completed in August of 1999 at the University of Tennessee, Knoxville, USA. As such, its contents reflect the result of many months of work conducted under the direction of several fine scholars. In particular, I am grateful to Professor Paul Davidson for serving as the director of my research and for the ongoing motivation and encouragement he has provided. His attention to detail and accuracy has resulted in a product of higher quality than I would have thought possible. It was his insistence that I submit my manuscript for publication that has led to it being presented in this format. For that, and for his conviction that there are civilized, ethical, and moral solutions to our economic problems, I express my deepest gratitude. Likewise, I express my thanks to Professor Hans Jensen, who is a true scholar, in every sense of the word. His love for teaching and his interest in his students are, in my experience, unequaled. Appreciation is also expressed to Professors Sydney Carroll and William Park for their advice and encouragement. Any errors, omissions, or oversights remaining in my work are due to my own shortcomings.

I am honored to be part of a community of Christian scholars, a community that has significantly influenced my work in a very positive way. My gratitude is expressed to the people of Milligan College for their support during my graduate studies at the University of Tennessee. The College's administration has steadfastly provided the support and working conditions necessary to complete my degree, for which I am thankful. I also wish to express my appreciation to the faculty of Milligan for their ongoing collegial support. I am especially grateful for the patience of the faculty of the Business Area. Their willingness to 'take up the slack' so that I could dedicate more time to my research was much appreciated. I wish to specifically thank Bob Mahan, my colleague and my friend, who, during many hours of conversation, has always expressed support for and interest in my work. Finally, I must also thank Professor Eugene Price, who remains in my mind the epitome of a 'gentle-man' and who provided my first serious exposure to economics.

To my parents, Jack and Virginia Greer, I offer my deepest thanks for instilling a love for God and a desire for education in my brothers and myself. I am also appreciative to them for raising me in a place like Mountain City, Tennessee, a place where ethical perspectives and moral values were the rule and not the exception. Finally, I thank my wife, Edwina, and my sons, Logan and Jeremy, who patiently tolerated all of my work 'on the computer in the big room'. Because of their understanding and encouragement, I have accomplished more than I would have dreamed possible. My hope is that this book, in some way, reflects the teaching and the values of those who have been such an important influence upon my life.

1. Background and direction

We live in a world full of contradiction and paradox, a fact of which perhaps the most fundamental illustration is this: that the existence of a problem of knowledge depends on the future being different from the past, while the possibility of the solution of the problem depends on the future being like the past.
Frank H. Knight (1921)[*]

With the development of a utilitarian ethics largely concerned with the summing up of consequences, the place of probability in ethical theory has become much more explicit ... the results of our endeavours are very uncertain ...
John M. Keynes (1921)

SHIFTING PARADIGMS

It has been said 'theorizing requires some notion of regularity or order' (Dow 1994, 196). Such a notion might be regarded as being fundamental to the acceptance of a paradigm in the Kuhnian[1] sense of research programs. Indeed, despite some debate to the contrary, Thomas Kuhn's theory of shifting paradigms is no less applicable to economics than to any other 'hard science'. In fact, his notion of 'normal science' as the mechanism of continuing research and study, or 'mopping up' by practitioners within any given field (Kuhn 1962, 24), certainly describes much of the evolution of economic thought. The propositions laid out by Adam Smith established the parameters within which the work of later economists was conducted. His advocacy of allowing the forces of self-interest and competition to function unimpeded by the external influence of governmental control led many other economists to build theories around these classical tenets. Ultimately, the body of work built upon these tenets drew these economists to believe that full employment would be the normal and expected outcome of such a system of free markets. Beginning in the early part of the twentieth century, however, when faced with the growing difficulty of maintaining full employment in a *laissez-faire* economy, some economists began to question the theory's underlying premises.

Kuhn points to the scientific revolution of Newtonian physics as an example of how paradigms shift as a result of ongoing research, as well as renewed examination of observable environmental characteristics, rather than through radically new discoveries. 'Newton's three laws of motion are less a product of novel experiments than of the attempt to reinterpret well-known observations in terms of the motions and interactions of primary neutral corpuscles' (Kuhn 1962, 104). The 'normal science' of continuing research and study within the established framework of economic theory eventually led economists, especially John Maynard Keynes, to question the validity of classical theory when applied to a modern economy.

During the early decades of the twentieth century, Keynes began to question the underlying logic of classical economic theory and its policy of *laissez-faire* that prescribed little if any government involvement in the economic affairs of society. In the classical view, the natural forces of supply and demand, combined with rationally behaving economic agents would result in a smoothly operating economy leading toward growth and prosperity for all. While policy makers continued to accept the tenets of classical theory well into the nineteenth and twentieth centuries and its accompanying development of a modern economy, society began to be burdened by worsening business cycles. Keynes succinctly states ' ... the outstanding faults of the economic society in which we live are its failure to provide for full employment and its arbitrary and inequitable distribution of wealth and incomes' (Keynes 1936, 372). His *General Theory* would, as Keynes himself said,

> ... argue that the postulates of the classical theory are applicable to a special case only and not the general case, the situation which it assumes being a limiting point of the possible positions of equilibrium. Moreover, the characteristics of the special case assumed by the classical theory happen not to be those of the economic society in which we actually live, with the result that its teaching is misleading and disastrous if we attempt to apply it to the facts of experience. (Keynes 1936, 3)

Frank Hyneman Knight, while regarded as a champion of the free market, shared in Keynes' criticism of the classical system, offering such observations as ' ... the present task is to show some of the reasons why, with the facts of nature, man, and society what they are, the framework of free enterprise does not at all imply an ideal social order' (Knight 1960, 97). Despite being intimately associated with the Chicago School of economic thought, Knight struggled throughout his life with the question of whether the prevailing orthodoxy of classical economic theorizing did, in fact, result in the most optimal and efficient allocation of resources in the quest to satisfy the unlimited wants and needs of a growing and changing society.

The prevailing concern of both Knight and Keynes was the achievement of an improved state of affairs for economic agents, both as individuals and as members of society. It is this distinction between the individual and society that brings about such a concern over the ethics of economics. More specifically, both Knight and Keynes were concerned about what they believed to be an endogenous component of the real world, but one missing from most economic analysis. That component was 'uncertainty'. They both recognized the potential conflict between actions taken for the good of oneself and actions taken for the good of society, with the result often being a less than socially optimal outcome. This result is worsened by the fact that individuals often simply do not know what the future will bring and therefore allow their decisions to be affected by apprehension and even undue conservatism about the future.

Keynes was especially concerned with how individuals respond to uncertainty in the decisions they make and the impact those decisions have upon employment, while Knight explored the impact of uncertainty on the creation of profit, wealth, and the distribution of income. While their emphases may differ, both men share a fundamental ethical and even moral concern about truth, liberty, and freedom of the individual. Their common concern, influenced as it was by the existence of uncertainty, was not often embraced by other, mainstream, economists.[2]

Still, to accuse most mainstream economists of failing to recognize the existence of uncertainty would perhaps be unfair. Indeed, most will readily admit that uncertainty exists in the daily life of every economic agent. The concept of uncertainty as a characteristic of the modern economy, however, is often replaced by the use of probabilistic risk, and the simple assumption that, in the long-run, the utility-maximizing decisions made by consumers and the profit maximizing decisions made by business entities will somehow result in the most efficient and socially beneficial allocation of our limited resources.[3] Frequently, in the long run, uncertainty is simply assumed away.

The concept of uncertainty within the field of economics has nonetheless been discussed, disputed, and investigated in a myriad of publications and from a number of points of view over the last several decades,[4] but over the course of this ongoing inquiry, the year 1921 serves as an extraordinary crossroads. It was in that year that Knight published his book *Risk, Uncertainty and Profit*, while Keynes' *A Treatise on Probability* also appeared for the first time in widespread publication. Both works deal, in a philosophical sense, with uncertainty and its impact upon economic decision making. Perhaps of greater significance is that both economists came to speak largely from opposing points of view. Knight was widely regarded as a major proponent of the free market, speaking out against efforts to increase political involvement in the economy, while Keynes was a well-known critic of *laissez-faire* and the classical economic theory[5] from which the notion sprang.

A recent article by David P. Levine suggests that 'uncertainty in economics arises in different contexts, but in all cases has to do with knowing and acting' (Levine 1997, 5). Whether the economic agent is an individual or a firm, the degree of knowledge available about possible future outcomes and their likelihood of occurrence affect the process of economic decision making. Both Knight and Keynes recognized that the amount and quality of information available plays a significant role in the sorts of decisions made. Knight was the first to make significant contributions to identifying uncertainty as the source of profit (Knight 1921a, 20). Keynes incorporated uncertainty into his criticism of *laissez-faire* by suggesting that uncertainty led economic agents to seek liquidity in the form of money balances held as security against an unknown and unpredictable future (Keynes 1936, 168).

However, to begin with a consideration of uncertainty as it relates solely to economic thinking is perhaps too confining. More generally, man has long battled with uncertainty, struggling to make decisions with incomplete or imperfect information regarding both the present and the future. A particularly well-known attempt to dispose of uncertainty entirely was made by René Descartes in 1628. Angered by those who claimed to prove that uncertainty could be overcome by probability, Descartes proceeded to show that virtually *anything* could be proven by the use of mathematics. Once a mathematical equation could be understood, it could remain accepted without doubt. For Descartes, if a postulate could be proven true through the established grounds of such a mathematical process, then it simply could not be held to be true. Such a practice brings individuals greater knowledge, and moves them closer to perfect certainty (Newbigin 1995, 20).

While few economists today believe that mathematical equations bring about perfect certainty, most would seem to agree that the existence of uncertainty poses no real complication for orthodox new classical or even new-Keynesian[6] economics. Knight and Keynes are among these few economists who place so much significance upon the concept of uncertainty. Not surprisingly then, much discussion, although little in-depth research, has ensued as to whether the views of Knight and Keynes with respect to questions of uncertainty are comparable or conflicting.

Despite fundamental differences in their respective concepts of uncertainty that surface after close examination, there are clear similarities upon which both economists build significant elements of their thinking.[7] Most important, the one thing that does remain clear is that both Knight and Keynes place uncertainty squarely at the center of their economics.[8] As such, it is appropriate to explore further the implication of this central theme upon their economic thinking and ultimately upon their ideas regarding economic policy. Of particular interest, and therefore the focus of this book, is the question of why two economists who gave uncertainty such a prominent position in their work could nonetheless arrive at such differing economic policy recommendations. Clearly, both economists shared similar concerns about ethics and uncertainty and the implication of each for economic theory. Further, both hoped to find ways in which economics could be used for the ultimate betterment of society, but upon closer examination, the stark contrast of the influences upon them, leading to contrasting views of reality, can be seen to account for much of this seeming paradox.

FRANK H. KNIGHT – THE SKEPTIC

There is little argument that Frank Knight played a crucial role in the birth and development of what Martin Bronfenbrenner has called the 'first' Chicago School of economic thought, referring to the collective body of economic theory emerging from the University of Chicago in the years prior to World War II. Bronfenbrenner suggests that the first Chicago School emphasized the influence of the price level more than the money supply and that the members of this school likewise showed a greater concern for 'the ethics and aesthetics of income and wealth ... [as well as] ... concern with economic freedom and allocative efficiency' (Bronfenbrenner 1962, 73). As a result of his influence upon the formation of the Chicago school, many of the most prominent economists of the twentieth (and the twenty-first) century point to Knight as a staunch supporter and advocate of *laissez-faire*.

Knight's acceptance of a free-market economy as the most socially optimal economic system, however, came only after years of study and thought and can be argued as being only marginally supportive of *laissez-faire*. Indeed, his advocacy of capitalism came about despite the fact that he recognized the existence of ethical and moral weaknesses within this form of economic system. In 1923, Knight remarked that 'discussion of the merits of free competition, or *laissez-faire*, takes on an especial interest in view of the contrast between the enticing plausibility of the case ... and the notoriously disappointing character of the results which it has tended to bring about in practice' (Knight 1923, 47) and in 1958 he said that 'by no means' is it proven 'that a policy of extreme governmental passivity (laisser faire) [sic] is the right or best solution for the general problems of economic relations. As we shall see, this is very far from being the case' (Knight 1960, 7).

Most analysis of Knight's work focuses on what many consider to be his zenith of thinking, the 1920s and 30s. Nonetheless, while Knight's 1921 *Risk, Uncertainty, and Profit* remains his most popular and perhaps most read publication, it is important to examine the overall scope of his life's work. This is especially true in the case of Knight, since he is known to have changed his opinion and point of view on a number of issues several times throughout his career, often preferring to take a moderate stance. In a 1936 review of a collection of Knight's essays published as *The Ethics of Competition*, C.E. Ayers, commenting about Knight's young age, says that 'we may therefore hope that he will some day give us a complete and mature statement of his social philosophy' and that the 'temptation to study the man behind the essays is irresistible' because 'what is most important about Knight as an economist is that he is also a philosopher' (Ayers 1936, 364). Knight's career is therefore made all the more intriguing because it represents many years of struggle over questions of economics, in particular the philosophical and ethical ramifications of the science.

While Knight eventually accepted the merits of a *laissez-faire* economic system and as a result proclaimed it to be the best choice for society, he never ceased from his criticism of its ethical and moral shortcomings. Therefore, it is important to consider not only his widely-known support for *laissez-faire*, but also his criticism of capitalism with specific attention paid to his ethical and moral objections, in particular his ongoing concern over social theory within a democratic system and the accompanying concept of individual freedom. Knight's emphasis upon matters of ethics became more obvious as his career progressed, with Knight becoming increasingly unsure that solutions to these shortcomings could be found (Schweitzer 1975, 289). While these growing ethical concerns were insufficient to sway Knight from his overall support of a free-market economy, they nonetheless provided him with a basis for supporting a limited, negative role for the government to play in the economic life of society.

JOHN M. KEYNES – THE OPTIMIST

While Knight went through life with a cynical, even pessimistic attitude, begrudgingly yet staunchly supportive of *laissez-faire*, Keynes 'loved life and sailed through it buoyant, at ease, and consummately successful, to become the architect of Capitalism Viable' (Heilbroner 1980, 251). Despite the suggestion that Keynes actually wanted to replace capitalism with some sort of centrally-planned economy, this is most assuredly not the case. As Robert Heilbroner has noted:

... it would be a grave error in judgment to place this man, whose aim was to rescue capitalism, in the camp of those who want to submerge it. True, he urged the 'socialization' of investment, although he was never very clear about what that meant; but if he sacrificed the part, it was to save the whole. (Heilbroner 1980, 276)

Keynes, while not seeking to destroy the principles of a free-market economy, was nonetheless a critic of classical economic theory. It was not the 'theory' of classical theory that he disputed. Rather, Keynes vehemently disagreed with certain underlying assumptions upon which the classical theories were built. Keynes himself points out that 'our criticism of the accepted classical theory of economics has consisted not so much in finding logical flaws in its analysis as in pointing out that its tacit assumptions are seldom or never satisfied, with the result that it cannot solve the economic problems of the actual world' (Keynes 1936, 378). In particular, Keynes recognized that money is not neutral,[9] that economic agents face an uncertain future and as a result may choose to hold money balances. Because of this, there may exist a period of insufficient effective demand to purchase the output of industry. As a result, periods of economic depression accompanied by high levels of involuntary unemployment can and do occur. Further, the market mechanism itself may be insufficient to correct this problem and government intervention in the economy may be necessary to bring about renewed economic growth and a return to higher levels of employment.

Like Knight, Keynes is of significant interest not only because of his economics but also because of his philosophy. O'Donnell suggests rightly, however, that most modern economists pay little attention to the philosophical foundations of Keynes. He writes, 'the key to more profound and comprehensive understandings of Keynes's thought is his *philosophy* ... for too long the illuminative power of this rich source of information has been neglected' (O'Donnell 1989, 3). He goes on to say that ' ... he was, in fact, far more influenced by philosophy than by economics in his early formative years; and during that period when both disciplines absorbed his attention, it is clear that philosophy rather than economics was his predominant love' (O'Donnell 1989, 11). Additionally, as an extension of his interest in philosophy, Keynes very much concerned himself with ethics, being heavily influenced by G.E. Moore's *Principia Ethica,* remaining 'an unreconstructed follower of G.E. Moore' (Skidelsky 1986, 104).

Keynes and Knight shared a remarkably similar interest in philosophy and ethics, as well as an obvious concern over the feasibility of classical economic theory and its resulting *laissez-faire* policy to provide an efficient, hospitable, economic environment. These similar interests, when combined with their common focus upon uncertainty as the basis for their economic theory, make it most interesting and appropriate to examine these two economists in light of one another. While accepting the prevailing recognition of Knight as a spokesman for *laissez-faire* and Keynes as its critic, it is interesting to observe the striking commonality of thought within much of their work. While this book does not attempt to mesh their thinking, it does attempt to highlight the significance of these similarities in regard to their ethical dimension while clarifying their points of convergence and their points of opposition.

PLAN OF THE BOOK

The approach taken will proceed first with a biographical and historical survey focusing upon aspects of their lives that apparently caused them to be so concerned about philosophy and ethics in the first place. Closer examination of the contrasting environments into which Knight and Keynes were born and raised will be conducted. Religious and intellectual influences upon both economists will also receive special attention.

Chapter 3 will provide consideration of the theories of uncertainty and the related concept of probability according to Knight and according to Keynes. Similarities and differences will be highlighted. The emphasis will be upon building sufficient understanding of this crucial aspect of their work to be able to analyze the issue in question – the ethical implications of uncertainty. It will be seen that their respective theories of probability reflect an important aspect of their view of reality, related to the ergodic or non-ergodic nature of the real world according to Knight and according to Keynes.

An analysis of Knight's and Keynes' specific ethical concerns over *laissez-faire*, classical economic thinking, and political economic theory follows in Chapter 4. This chapter will emphasize the ethical ramifications of uncertainty as well as the centrality each economist bestows upon it. Included will be some consideration of certain aspects of their respective conceptualized realities[10] of the economic world, including uncertainty, and their accompanying social structure, revealing a further basis for their ethical concerns and criticisms.

Next, Chapter 5 will focus upon fundamental similarities and differences in their ideas regarding the purpose and method of economics. Given Knight's and Keynes' emphasis on the ethical and philosophical aspects of the science, it is important to understand what each believed the purpose of economics to be and, more important, how it could be used to improve the quality of life for individuals and for society. The ramifications of seeing economics as merely an analytical mechanism as opposed to seeing economics as a tool to be used in developing economic policy will be investigated.

It will be seen in Chapter 6 that, given the diversity of the environmental influences upon them, their opposing views of reality, as well as differences in their points of view regarding the purpose of economics, it is no surprise that they developed such contrasting, yet compromising, economic policy recommendations. The divergence of their proposals, the contrast in their outlooks for the future, as well as their resignation to a 'middle way' will be discussed.

Finally, Chapter 7 closes the investigation with an overview of what has been learned from the process of examining these important issues, with special emphasis upon the impact of Knight's and Keynes' opposing views of reality. The results indicate that the backgrounds and influences upon both Knight and Keynes greatly affected their views of reality and were critical factors in the development of their theories of uncertainty and resulting views regarding the role of economic theory itself. Despite some commonality in their respective focus upon, and theories of, uncertainty, when combined with opposing views of reality and their opinions regarding the role and purpose of economics, the results are dramatically different economic world views and concomitant policy recommendations. Nonetheless, perhaps the most significant conclusion of all is that both of these important twentieth-century economists maintained a life-long desire to bring about improvement to society.

Figure 1.1 illustrates the overall organization of the study set forth in this book. The first step is to build an initial understanding of key influential elements that were part of their early, developmental years, in particular those that drove both Knight and Keynes toward economic and ethical concerns. From this foundation, their respective views of reality will be considered from the perspective of their notions about probability and uncertainty.

These elements, combined with the views of Knight and Keynes on the purpose and role of economic theory, will facilitate a better understanding of their divergent economic outlooks and policy recommendations. Throughout the investigation, the focus will remain on ethical concerns, which served as a common influence upon both Knight and Keynes, directing them to develop theories and policies that each believed would improve the economic condition of man.

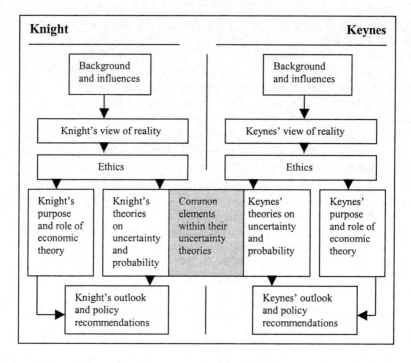

Figure 1.1 The place of uncertainty in the economics of Keynes and Knight

NOTES

* The quotations at the opening of the chapters are not intended to be academic citations, but are representative of the author's thinking at the time of the quote. Therefore, the respective dates do not necessarily relate to specific references in the bibliography.

1. Thomas Kuhn's *The Structure of Scientific Revolutions* (1962) explored the idea that old paradigms give way to new paradigms when scientists, researchers, or academics sufficiently question the fundamental axioms of the prevailing paradigm. This 'revolution' results in a new way of looking at problems in question, including new sorts of research techniques and methods.

2. The term 'mainstream economists' refers to those economists who recognize and function within the widely accepted 'orthodox' paradigms prevalent within what is referred to as new classical (stressing neoclassical precepts) and new-Keynesian (or simply Keynesian) economic theory.

3. This is the logical conclusion of the use of probabilistic analysis in which the long-run results in an infinitely large sample and, therefore, an insignificantly small standard deviation. Indeed, observations in this size sample would be equivalent to the mean.

4. See especially Shackle, Davidson, Hey, Levine, Schmidt, Weintraub, O'Donnell, and Lawson.

5. Keynes' own definition in *The General Theory* of the school of thought regarded as 'classical' states: '"The classical economists" was a name invented by Marx to cover

Ricardo and James Mill and their *predecessors*, that is to say for the founders of the theory which culminated in the Ricardian economics. I have become accustomed, perhaps perpetrating a solecism, to include in "the classical school" the *followers* of Ricardo, those, that is to say, who adopted and perfected the theory of the Ricardian economics, including (for example) J.S. Mill, Marshall, Edgeworth and Prof. Pigou' (Keynes 1936, 3n).

6. New-Keynesian economics refers to that school of thought which purports to accurately interpret Keynes by including such elements as price and wage rigidity in its foundational assumptions.

7. See Chapter 3 for detailed discussion of these similarities and differences and Chapter 4 for an examination of their ethical implications.

8. Robert Skidelsky writes in his authoritative biography of Keynes 'there should have been some points of sympathy between Knight and Keynes. Knight was the first to point to the pervasiveness of uncertainty in economic affairs, and to distinguish properly between "uncertainty" and "risk"'(Skidelsky 1986, vol 1, 577).

9. Central to the acceptance of classical economic theory is the idea that money serves merely as a medium of exchange, the logical conclusion of Say's Law.

10. The term 'conceptualized reality' refers to the association of economic actors, institutions, and relationships in formulating a model of the 'real world' as perceived in the mind of an economist.

2. Contrasting theological and intellectual influences

> *Ethics is a subject about which there has been and still is an immense amount of difference of opinion, in spite of all the time and labour which have been devoted to the study of it.*
>
> G.E. Moore

ETHICAL INFLUENCES

As a first step in examining the ethical[1] basis of Knight's and Keynes' economic thinking, it is appropriate to begin by developing a thorough understanding of significant influences upon that thinking. The risk of such an undertaking is that the resulting product will merely echo what has been done before. After all, much has already been widely published exploring the many influences upon Keynes.[2] This is much less true of Knight, even though a few scholars have produced a reasonable and growing quantity of scholarly research.[3]

Knight has long been viewed as an economist with a strong philosophical perspective. His concern with utilitarianism as it related to the ultimate structure of society led him to propose that the problems of man were moral rather than economic. He asked, 'it is one thing to ask what is Good, and another to inquire as to what social policy is to be carried out, and by what agencies, in order to realize the Good as far as possible' (Knight 1947a, 1). As a result of this and many other such interrogatories, much of the research surrounding him and his work focuses upon such philosophical issues. While some recent interest has been expressed in the philosophy of Keynes,[4] focusing largely upon the influence of Moore and others, such a perspective is certainly the exception and not the rule, with significantly more attention paid to the macroeconomic and monetary theory aspects of his work.

With the ultimate purpose of this book being to explore the ethical basis for and contrasting ramifications of uncertainty in the work of Knight and

Keynes, it is appropriate, nonetheless, to begin with a survey of significant influences upon their thinking. This book will limit its examination to those influences that most affected the formation of Knight's and Keynes' ethical perspectives. In particular, our efforts will focus upon theological and intellectual influences that affected the development of their respective 'world views' or 'conceptualized realities' and their concomitant policy recommendations.

THEOLOGY – THE CALL TO COMMUNITY

A logical starting point in this examination is to consider the issue of theology and, more specifically, the role theology plays in the lives of individuals and of society. Theology provides perhaps the most important foundational element in shaping one's ethics, whether a particular theological view is accepted or not. While acceptance of one theological tenet or another may provide the basis for a particular ethical perspective, it may be the lack of a theological view that shapes another.

The development of economic thought has itself been significantly influenced by religion. In fact, theologians have long attempted to direct economic thinking and economic policy by decreeing the church's position on various economic activities. During the latter years of the middle ages the Catholic Church became increasingly concerned that the market system was beginning to have a significant influence upon society. The resulting debate over the 'just price' of a good and the practice of 'usury' had a pronounced affect on economic development for centuries to come. According to R.H. Tawney,

> ... not only the taking of interest for a loan, but the raising of prices by a monopolist, the beating down of prices by a keen bargainer ... the excessive profits of a middleman – all these had been denounced as usury ...the truth is, indeed, that any bargain, in which one party obviously gained more advantage than the other, and used his power to the full, was regarded as usurious. (Tawney 1962, 153)

By the 1500s, the Protestant reformers had recognized the growing chasm between the established church and the people. Increasing economic activity forced John Calvin and his followers to propose a new theology in terms of economic life. Tawney observes,

> ... it is not that they abandon the claim of religion to moralize economic life, but that the life which they are concerned to moralize is one in which the main features of a commercial civilization are taken for granted, and that it is for

application to such conditions that their teaching is designed. Early Calvinism
… has its own rule, and a rigorous rule, for the conduct of economic affairs …
its ideal is a society which seeks wealth with the sober gravity of men who are
conscious at once of disciplining their own characters by patient labor, and of
devoting themselves to a service acceptable to God. (Tawney 1962, 105)

According to Calvin's teaching, ' … the idleness of the mendicant was both a
sin against God and a social evil; the enterprise of the thriving tradesman was
at once a Christian virtue and a benefit to the community' (Tawney 1962,
115).

As economic thought developed further into the eighteenth and nineteenth
centuries, the theological and ethical aspects of economic life took on a role
of secondary importance to the primary role of rigorous marginal analysis
and empirical testing. Still, the ethical conflict of individual self-interest
versus social welfare never disappears completely. Indeed, of particular
interest to Knight and Keynes were the ethical ramifications of making
economic decisions as self-interested members of society. As has been
observed, questions regarding the ethics of individual versus society have
often been addressed via theological and philosophical inquiry. Theology
after all functions beyond the realm of the individual, extending to matters of
community, society, and collective matters of faith and belief. It concerns
itself in part with the role of individuals within such a community.
Furthermore, both theological and ethical views often stem from influences
present early in life. The developmental years of both Knight and Keynes are
no exception.

By necessity, a study of the early years and development of any particular
individual must include some observation and analysis of the context of their
childhood and developmental years. In the case of Knight and Keynes, this is
most assuredly a study in contrasts. While Knight was born into a mid-
western family of modest means and conservative thinking, Keynes was born
into educated and influential British affluence. In both cases, nonetheless,
their environments were shaped by the influence of similar, yet divergent
sources. Specifically, both of their worlds were presently, or had recently
been, dominated by a tenuous adherence to an evangelical religion that
seemed to support the prevailing schools of economic thought. In the case of
Keynes, the established paradigm of *laissez-faire* reigned supreme.
Individualism, based upon one's pursuit of self-interest, was protected by the
belief that a free and uncontrolled market would be self-regulating because of
the inherent goodness of man, a moral and ethical construct of Enlightenment
thinkers, not the least of whom was Adam Smith. In the case of Knight, born
into an America barely 100 years old, the frontier was itself a product of
individual rights. The very existence of exploitable resources such as vast

expanses of fertile land was evidence of God's blessing upon those individuals brave and bold enough to stake out a claim.

Nonetheless, in England during the latter part of the nineteenth century, the conflict between the metaphysics of theology and the hard sciences of the Enlightenment reached a crisis point, leading to the eventual demise of religious belief among Cambridge intellectuals. The same could not be said of the American mid-west, however, where churches and evangelists continued to promote strict adherence to Biblical scripture (Fogde 1977, 156).

Keynes himself was the product of a family with deeply religious roots. Skidelsky's biography points to much evidence of this, taken primarily from the diary of Keynes' father, Neville. Maynard Keynes' paternal grandfather, John Keynes, was widely regarded as a successful businessman. 'As he prospered, John Keynes diversified into banking and other commercial activities. Like most self-made Victorian businessmen he attributed his success in life to hard work and religious principles' (Skidelsky 1986, 5).

After the birth of Keynes' father, religious training and support continued to be provided by the household, with Neville's father promoting faith in a 'good Jesus' and his grandmother sitting ' ... all day with a Bible on her knee, mouthing the words of the scriptures' (Skidelsky 1986, 6). This devoutly religious attitude apparently did not remain with Neville into his adulthood. With universities suddenly faced with the responsibilities of providing a broad, scientifically-based education in the new industrial era to students possessing a decreasing religious faith and growing intellectual aptitude, Neville began studies in the moral sciences.[5] In fact, ' ... parts of the moral sciences – especially moral and political philosophy and political economy – were coming to be seen as a source of social wisdom, replacing some of the functions hitherto performed by religion'. Most importantly, 'Neville's switch to moral sciences determined the atmosphere in which Maynard Keynes was to grow up. He was a product of the Cambridge moral science tradition, in which Cambridge economics developed side by side with Cambridge moral philosophy' (Skidelsky 1986, 10).

The Cambridge School of Economics, which was heavily influenced by John Stuart Mill, was '... Benthamite in that aspect of its thought which related to social policy. Mill's Utilitarianism, Cambridge mathematics, and Cambridge's Nonconformist conscience were the chief constituents in what became the Cambridge School of Economics, whose founder was Alfred Marshall' (Skidelsky 1986, 31). As for Cambridge moral philosophy, '... there were two main traditions ... for the post-theological intellectuals to draw on: Intuitionism and Utilitarianism. Both had theological roots, but were capable of non-theological development, because both started with an appeal to human reason.' There were ' ... two different aspects of human reason ... being appealed to: in the first case, what might loosely be called conscience; in the second case, calculation. Both presupposed certain kinds of knowledge: Intuitionism, moral knowledge produced by a moral faculty; Utilitarianism, knowledge of consequences' (Skidelsky 1986, 28).

So it was that John Maynard Keynes was born into an era of religious and intellectual tension, a tension that his father had succumbed to by immersing himself in the moral sciences. This replacement for religion provided the social scientists of the day with justification for their work. They could claim that economic decisions should be based upon the goodness of man, a man with free will who could and should direct his own actions. Rather than actions being dictated by the rigidity of religion and scriptural teaching, individuals should be allowed to make decisions for themselves. Believing in the inherent goodness of man provided ethicists, moralists, and economists alike with an argument for free markets in which the natural order of things would assure a smoothly operating, hospitable social environment.

As for the American mid-west of the late 1800s, the story was different. The post-Civil War era, in particular, was marked by the general attitude that God blessed the citizens of the United States with vast material resources ripe for exploitation. Americans became committed to a sort of individualistic religion, as well as to the pursuit of economic and social reward, all provided by the hand of God (Fogde 1977, 4).

America was, however, dominated by what has been called ' ... two religions, or at least two different forms of the same religion [with] the prevailing Protestant ideology [representing] a syncretistic mingling of the two' (Mead 1963, 135). The two religions were

> ... the religion of the denominations, which was commonly articulated in the terms of scholastic Protestant orthodoxy and almost universally practiced in terms of ... pietistic revivalism ... [and] ... the religion of the democratic society and nation. This was rooted in the rationalism of the Enlightenment ... and was articulated in terms of the destiny of America, under God, to be fulfilled by perfecting the democratic way of life for the example and betterment of all mankind. (Mead 1963, 135)

Born in 1885, Knight reveals that 'as a toddler, I toddled under a Republican table, on a farm in the Middle West' (Knight 1960, 6). The significance of this is twofold. First, it goes without saying that being raised in a Republican household will, or one would assume should, have a pronounced influence on one's way of thinking. In many cases, the tendency is to follow in this conservative mind-set. In other cases, the opposite is true. Knight's acceptance of free-market capitalism would suggest that he carried his family's conservative thinking with him throughout his career. First, it must be remembered that Knight did not accept a free-market economy without question. Knight's evolving ideas regarding society, individual freedom, and problems arising from within human nature left him much room in which to criticize *laissez-faire*. Second, being born in the mid-west, Knight spent his most formative years within a religiously conservative geographic region of the United States at a time when evangelism was at its peak and Puritanical thinking permeated much of society.

Inevitably these two forces combined to instill in Knight an awareness of right and wrong as well as a critical eye for the ethical and moral aspects within virtually every issue of concern. Additionally, Knight's parents were members of the conservative wing of the independent Christian Church movement, the Disciples of Christ.[6] Their bond to the church was strong. Several of Knight's male relatives, including his grandfather were ordained ministers (Dewey 1986, 12). Knight was undoubtedly the recipient of many sermons from the pulpit of a church that was largely based upon highly conservative fundamentalist principles. Knight's student, George Stigler, retells a story obtained from Knight's younger brother:

> Under the urging of their deeply religious parents, on one Sunday the numerous children signed pledges to attend church the rest of their lives. On returning home, Frank, then fourteen or fifteen, assembled the younger children behind the barn, built a small fire, and said, 'Burn these things because pledges and promises made under duress are not binding'. (Stigler 1988, 181)

Knight's close ties to the church nonetheless continued when he began his college years at American University in Harriman, Tennessee, which was affiliated with the Disciples of Christ Church. Knight left American University in 1907 and moved on to Milligan College in Johnson City, Tennessee in 1908 which, at that time, was also affiliated with the Disciples of Christ. While there, he studied ethics and religion along with a program of classical studies. Even at the University of Tennessee, where Knight continued his education immediately after graduation from Milligan, students were required to attend chapel on a daily basis (Dewey 1986, 38).

It is no surprise then that Knight carried with him a strong concern for ethics, at the very least an awareness of right and wrong, and that virtually every issue he explored was done so, mindful of its ethical influences and ramifications. Knight reacted with rebellion to this inundation of religious doctrine, eventually adopting the viewpoint of secular humanism and becoming critical of the role played by the church in modern society. Replacing Knight's early Christian faith is 'a profound skepticism, which is the principal ingredient in Knight's political and economic conservatism' (McKinney 1977, 1438). Perhaps not surprisingly, Knight eventually grew to question even religion itself proclaiming that 'I wake up in the middle of the night and think about religion. It's that damned religion. I can't get it out of my mind' (Dewey 1986, 2).

THEOLOGY VERSUS ENLIGHTENED THINKING

The worlds into which Keynes and Knight were born differed significantly in the way in which society viewed theology and its role in providing moral authority. In the case of Keynes, Cambridge of the late 1800s was the center of a philosophical crossroads in which theology was gradually being replaced by more scientifically-based views regarding both creation and conduct. Interestingly, while economics had long been seen, from the classical perspective, as a science based upon self-interest and Benthamite utilitarianism, it was, nonetheless, economics that surfaced as a replacement for theology. It was Keynes' teacher, Alfred Marshall, who succeeded in developing economics into a sort of ethical and even moral authority that possessed the scientific basis theology lacked and for which Cambridge academicians craved (Skidelsky 1986, 40).

Nonetheless, Marshall was not entirely successful in promoting economics as the sole moral guide for both individual decision and social policy making. A philosophical struggle remained over how Benthamite-based utilitarian economics might ensure the good of society, based as it was upon a maximization of individual pleasure and a minimization of individual pain. This conflict required the participation of people beyond those primarily concerned with economics. The discussion of their contribution follows in the next section.

In the absence of a common commitment to religion and a God who rewarded good, sympathetic behavior, there was a void to be filled in regard to a sense of community and belonging that had previously been provided by allegiance to a common God. The University took this role upon itself. The University became a community of scholars who promoted adherence to a high standard of moral values that was taken as seriously as the educational process itself (Mini 1991, 58). This sharing of common values created a sense of community and social responsibility that was necessary if Utilitarian economics was to be allowed to go unchecked.

While the centers of higher learning in America were, like those of England, struggling with the lack of empirical evidence supporting theological views, in his early years Knight was far removed from such controversy. In the conservative, rural mid-west, the evangelical efforts of multiple denominations were in high gear, spreading the word of repentance and salvation to a widely-dispersed, but rapidly growing population. Despite growing doubts about religion among American academics, the growing affluence of the century-old nation was touted by many industrialists, and by many evangelists, as being a blessing from God. Andrew Carnegie, a prime example of this new industrial and commercial wealth did not hesitate to use religious imagery and justification for his great accumulation of wealth. He pronounced:

> This, then, is held to be the duty of the man of wealth; To set an example of modest, unostentatious living, shunning display or extravagance; to provide moderately for the legitimate wants of those dependent upon him; and, after doing so, to consider all surplus revenues which come to him simply as trust funds, which he is called upon to administer, and strictly bound as a matter of duty to administer in the manner which, in his judgment, is best calculated to produce the most beneficial results for the community – the man of wealth thus becoming the mere trustee and agent for his poorer brethren, bringing to their service his superior wisdom, experience, and ability to administer, doing for them better than they would or could do for themselves. (Fogde 1977, 44)

Many clergy of the day proclaimed the blessing of God upon the industrious. The Reverend Russell Conwell not only claimed the blessings of God upon the rich, but the condemnation of God upon the poor. He made these points during hundreds of sermons:

> Money is power, and you ought to be reasonably ambitious to have it. You ought because you can do more good with it than you could without it ... if you can honestly attain unto riches ... it is your Christian and Godly duty to do so ... there is not a poor person in the United States who was not made poor by his own shortcomings, or by the shortcomings of someone else. It is all wrong to be poor, anyhow ... to sympathize with a man whom God has punished for his sins, thus to help him when God would still continue a just punishment, is to do wrong, no doubt about it, and we do that more than we help those who are deserving. (Fogde 1977, 48)

Not only does Knight grow up in a religiously conservative family in a religiously conservative part of the world, but he attended religiously conservative institutions of higher education. Nonetheless, it is during his college years that Knight comes to terms with his distaste of American evangelical religion and grows more and more skeptical in regard to its ultimate value. Unlike Keynes, who naturally developed a world view devoid of theological underpinnings, supported by a community of like-minded souls, Knight developed his criticism of theology in spite of family and educational influences committed to evangelical religion.

Knight's struggle with theology did not come from its message that God blessed the industrious. Rather, Knight reacted negatively to those theologians who were critical of the growing inequalities of wealth and income distribution. Knight was fearful that their messages would somehow interfere with the workings of a capitalistic, free-market economy. Knight believed that 'the greater danger from Christian ethics lies in the tendency to carry the sentimental, brotherhood morality of primitive tribal life – more especially the condemnation of differences in wealth and power, which are organizational conditions of efficiency – into practical measures of internal social reform to such an extent, or in such ways, as to work serious injury' (Knight and Merriam 1945, 95).

Knight came to recognize that economics, not religion, would provide the best solution to the inherent conflicts between decision making for the benefit of a single individual and decision making for the good of society (Knight and Merriam 1945, 98). This conclusion, however, does not mean that Knight's work was no longer affected by religion. Indeed, his work, as that of Keynes, continued to bear the mark of theological influence.

INTELLECTUAL INFLUENCES – PHILOSOPHER ECONOMISTS

Just as their theological environments and resulting influences differed, so did the intellectual development of Keynes and Knight. Hardly a greater contrast could exist than that between the cultural and intellectual worlds of rural mid-America and Cambridge England at the turn of the last century. As has already been suggested, Cambridge arguably represented the center of British academic life. In fact, it is fair to say that Cambridge was very much the crossroads of a dying adherence to theology and religion as the provider of moral and social direction and a growing infatuation with science as a replacement. Rural America, on the other hand, clung to religion as a primary justification for expansion and industrialization. The worlds of theological and intellectual influence are bound up together in this ongoing, ethically-based philosophical discussion.

Keynes was obviously the product of a community of scholars who were devoted to working out the problems of life using logic, science, and rational thinking. At the same time, the struggle between theology as the bastion of moral value and the rationality of man resulted in much agonized debate. Put into vivid historical context by Skidelsky, ' ... the 1860s were the decade when Cambridge men lost their religious faith: Edward Carpenter, Leslie Stephen, Henry Sidgwick, Alfred Marshall, Arthur Balfour were all from the "doubting class" of the 1860s.' This decade of decisive change began with the publishing of Darwin's *Origin of Species* in 1859, the consequences of which were as far reaching as perhaps any book before or since. 'Occurring more or less simultaneously, the death of God, and the birth of mass democracy wonderfully concentrated men's minds on the problems of social order and personal conduct' (Skidelsky 1986, 26).

One cannot dismiss this conflict of theology and reason as an inconsequential or irrelevant influence upon Keynes. With his father intimately tied to the university and his teachers Henry Sidgwick and Alfred Marshall, Keynes spent much of his life in close proximity to the ongoing battles for university reform that occurred in response to the clash of social and moral philosophy. Within the Keynes household, as within many others, religion came to be replaced by reason as the determinant of good conduct of both the individual and of society. The remaining problem was reconciliation of the two.

O'Donnell claims ' ... he [Keynes] was ... far more influenced by philosophy than by economics in his early formative years ... it is clear that philosophy, rather than economics was his dominant love' (O'Donnell 1989, 11). It is Moore, and his *Principia Ethica* that was perhaps the most dominant intellectual influence upon the young Keynes. Keynes' tutelage under Moore, combined with his personal involvement with the Apostles,[7] provided intimate contact with and exposure to Moore's philosophical approach to ethics.

The influence of Moore must be considered, however, in light of the failure of Henry Sidgwick to fully reconcile the opposing philosophical forces of theology and reason in guiding individual and social decision making. Sidgwick identified the reconciliation of 'the two species of hedonism ... Universalistic and Egoistic' as the fundamental problem to be solved within the study of ethics (Sidgwick 1874, 497). Sidgwick took Universalitic Hedonism to be the sort 'taught by Bentham and his successors, that is more generally understood under the term "Utilitarianism"' (Sidgwick 1874, 11). Further, Egoistic Hedonism or simply 'Egoism' is understood by Sidgwick to be ' ... a system which prescribes actions as means to the end of the individual's happiness or pleasure' (Sidgwick 1874, 89). Unfortunately, Sidgwick was unable to reconcile the two successfully, concluding ' ... it seems, then, that we must conclude ... that the inseparable connexion [sic] between Utilitarian Duty and the greatest happiness of the individual who conforms to it cannot be satisfactorily demonstrated on empirical grounds' (Sidgwick 1874, 503).

It seems to make no sense to Sidgwick that individuals would act for altruistic reasons other than selfish ones unless a God who would reward such behavior did, in fact, exist. He could find no empirical evidence for this, however, and in the new-found Cambridge tradition therefore dismissed such ideas. ' ... I cannot find inseparably connected with this conviction, and similarly attainable by mere reflective intuition, any cognition that there actually is a Supreme Being who will adequately reward me for obeying these rules of duty,[8] or punish me for violating them' (Sidgwick 1874, 507). Sidgwick's inability to reconcile social and moral philosophy left an opportunity for someone else – G.E. Moore – to do so.

The impact both of Moore's writings and his own membership in the Apostles upon the ultimate ethical thinking of Keynes was significant. It was Moore who was able to provide a sense of justification to the Apostles and their proclivity to separate themselves from the Cambridge community at large only to form close bonds of friendship among themselves, bonds that filled a void left from a dwindling religious faith. Indeed, it was Moore who claimed that 'ethics' is based upon a discussion of 'good' and 'bad'. 'Good' to Moore was undefinable, but included such things as the appreciation of beauty and the pleasure gained from friendship and community (Moore 1903, 17). Moore's emphasis upon friendship and community as well as his generally negative comments regarding Benthamite Utilitarianism led the Apostles and Keynes to receive his *Principia Ethica* with great excitement (Mini 1991, 67).

Mini points out perhaps the clearest connection between Moore and his influence upon the later work of Keynes. In identifying Moore's obsession with 'coldly analysing every sentence, every work, ferreting out ambiguities, making distinctions ... ' (Mini 1991, 70), he illustrates Moore's predilection for questioning anything in which he finds even slight ambiguity or logical flow. This underlies Keynes' struggle with the precepts of classical economics in light of the great economic upheavals of the early twentieth century. By bringing into question the validity of Say's Law Keynes uses Moore's method of questioning what no one else had questioned before. By pointing out the inherent fallacies of previously accepted axioms, Keynes opened the door to a new approach in economic analysis (Mini 1991, 71).

While scholars have rightly identified Keynes' interest in and even fascination with Moore's work, it is also correct to suggest that *Principia Ethica* not only led Keynes toward what would become his *Treatise on Probability*, which ellucidates the development of his own thinking on probability, but also led him to a growing concern for the ethical ramifications of uncertainty. This line of thinking will be further explored in the following chapter. Keynes continued his fascination with philosophy throughout the first decade or so of the twentieth century, reading the work of people such as Brentano, Cournot, and the man whom Keynes called 'the superb Hume' (O'Donnell 1989, 14).

Compared to Keynes, who was able to absorb the intellectual influences of Marshall, Moore and the Apostles while sitting in their midst, Knight would surely be considered a self-made intellectual. The religious teachings and dogma of his day directly influenced him, first as a child through regular church attendance and as a member of a conservative, religious family, then as a student at evangelical institutions of higher education. Despite this close association with theology, Knight adopted a well-known skepticism toward religion. Knight, despite the influence of virtually everyone around him, and as a result of considerable struggle, adopted a more scientific view of the world, just as Keynes had done through osmosis of his environment.

While the formal education of Keynes at home, at Eton, and at Cambridge has been well documented,[9] the same cannot be said of Knight. With the exception of fairly recent research into Knight's early years,[10] little has been widely published. This omission does not, however, make his educational history any less interesting. In fact, of particular interest at present is the consideration of how two individuals with such contrasting educational and cultural backgrounds could, nonetheless, come to be known for their highly intellectual treatments of economics in general and uncertainty in particular.

Unlike Keynes, whose early formative years at home were shaped by formally educated intellectual parents and whose own formal education was obtained from the most highly regarded of British academic institutions, Knight's own education was hardly impressive. In fact, it has been called a 'strange educational career dictated by the family's poverty' (Stigler 1988, 181).

Dewey recounts the circuit followed by Knight from his farmhouse in McLean County, Illinois to his ultimate arrival at Cornell University. What few records exist suggest that Knight did not complete his high-school education because of the demands placed upon him by his father and the family farm, not an uncommon prioritization in the agricultural mid-west. Nonetheless, Knight committed himself to study and was able to prepare himself for college even without completion of his secondary education (Dewey 1986, 11).

It was previously mentioned that Knight's early education was at religiously conservative institutions, including American University, a small, unheard-of college in East Tennessee, where Knight enrolled in 1905. While there, Knight received 'the high school education he had failed to receive because of the demands placed upon his earlier education by his father's need for labourers on the farm' (Emmett 1990, 119). It was at American that Knight encountered Frederick Kershner, who taught numerous subjects at American, and who quickly became a mentor for Knight. American closed in 1908 and Kershner moved to Milligan College, also in East Tennessee, to become its president. Knight went with him (Emmett 1990, 126).

While Milligan was an equally small and equally evangelical institution, it did provide Knight with a broad-based, liberal-arts education with exposure to classical history and literature as well as foreign language, science, mathematics, and of course, religion (Dewey 1986, 20). During his years as an undergraduate at Milligan, Knight professed an outward adherence to the religious dogma pronounced by the school, despite the evidence that he was already developing a deep skepticism about theology in general and established religion in particular. Despite these growing doubts, Knight continued to write for conservative journals and to incorporate pro-religion rhetoric into occasional addresses given to the student body (Emmett 1990, 120). Nevertheless, it is clear that the seeds of what would become considerable criticism directed toward religion had been sown.

Knight moved with his wife[11] to Knoxville and the University of Tennessee following their graduation from Milligan in 1911 (Dewey 1986, 23). Even though the administration at Tennessee initially questioned the merit of Knight's undergraduate studies, it was soon evident that American and especially Milligan had prepared him well. Consistently earning high grades, Knight went on to study the natural sciences (earning a B.Sc.) as well as foreign languages and history (earning an M.A.). His exposure to the sciences taught him to view the world critically, with an eye toward the development of provable hypotheses, while his exposure to foreign languages and history led him to develop interest in sociological issues. This combination of interests was not uncommon among 'thinkers emerging from Protestant backgrounds at this time, and Knight's decision to move into the social sciences seems to have been motivated by concerns similar to many of his socially progressive contemporaries' (Emmett 1990, 134).

Knight next moved to Cornell University, where he initially studied philosophy. However, at the insistence of the faculty in the department, he transferred to economics where he studied with Alvin Johnson. Emmett identifies this change as being the result of his philosophy professor's[12] belief that Knight was simply not intended for the study of philosophy (Emmett 1990, 143). It was, in fact, not simply Knight's perceived inappropriateness for philosophy that troubled his professors. Rather, his professors were troubled by Knight's attempts to show that 'human experience cannot be made intelligible by attempts to define it either in completely objective or completely subjective terms' (Emmett 1990, 148). Knight sought to determine a way in which both the objective and the subjective could be considered in the examination of social issues. The failure of the Cornell philosophy faculty to understand his desire to identify the 'partial truth' in both objective and subjective views ultimately resulted in Knight's completion of his doctorate in economics, rather than philosophy.

Knight, unlike Keynes, was never surrounded by 'great' intellectuals or original thinkers. Certainly, his friendship with Frederick Kershner, his years at the University of Tennessee, as well as his Cornell encounters with professors such as Creighton and Johnson provided Knight with intellectual stimulation and academic rigor. Still, much of the philosophical and ethical influences upon Knight are not from his personal encounters, but from his readings of such innovative classical economists as Adam Smith and Karl Marx and from philosophers such as William James and Henry Bergson. In fact, it is from James that Knight's pluralism[13] is derived, while he develops his own ideas of emergent evolution[14] from Bergson (McKinney 1977, 1439). Despite this rather circuitous route from rural Illinois, through the mountains of East Tennessee, and on to Cornell, Knight ultimately puts his education, both formal and self-taught, to use as he proves to be a pioneer in the creation of Bronfenbrenner's 'first' Chicago School of Economics.

NOTES

1. The term 'ethics', which will be used frequently throughout this book, is taken to mean, in the words of John Dewey, 'the science that deals with conduct, in so far as this is considered as right or wrong, good or bad ... another way of stating the same thing is to say that Ethics aims to give a systematic account of our judgments about conduct, in so far as these estimate it from the standpoint of right or wrong, good or bad' (Dewey 1908, 1).
2. Certainly Roy Harrod's *Life* served for over thirty years as the authoritative biography of Keynes until Robert Skidelsky's comprehensive two-volume biography appeared in 1986 and 1992. A third volume is forthcoming. Many others have also produced significant research on Keynes.
3. For the most part, Knight has been widely documented primarily as an influence upon other, more popular, Chicago School economists of the twentieth century such as Milton Friedman and George Stigler. No comprehensive, authoritative biography exists to this day, largely because he sought recognition among scholars, not the general public. Stigler says of Knight, 'devotion to knowledge was exemplified and its message reinforced by Knight's way of life. He was not a consultant to great bodies or small, whether public or private; he did not ride the lecture circuit; he did not seek a place in the popular press. He conducted himself as if the pursuit of academic knowledge was a worthy fulltime career for a first-class mind' (Stigler 1988, 18). Ross B. Emmett and Stephen J. Nash are among those conducting recent scholarly research on Knight.
4. In particular, the work of O'Donnell, Carabelli, and others.
5. The Moral Science Tripos was composed of studies in moral philosophy, political philosophy, logic, psychology, and economics.
6. The Disciples of Christ was regarded as the more conservative wing of the Christian Church, Church of Christ movement. The movement was collectively known to promote the precepts set forth by it founders, Alexander Campbell and Barton Stone. While the movement claimed no denominational status, there remained a loose association among the churches. Differences of opinion regarding certain theological issues, such as the use of musical instruments, brought division among the movement, resulting in the emergence of three basic sub-groups. The Christian Churches were regarded as the most mainstream, while the Churches of Christ and the Disciples of Christ were more religiously conservative. The Disciples, nonetheless, were more ecumenical, seeking unity among the various divisions of the Stone–Campbell movement (see Allen and Hughes, and McLoughlin).
7. The Apostles, or the Cambridge Conversazione Society, was the most elite campus organization at the University, boasting many members who had gone on to have significant influence upon the cultural and political fortunes of England. Membership was strictly limited and members shared common interests in academia, literature, and philosophy as well as a common disdain for the world outside their circle.

8. Such 'Rules of Duty' included those actions that resulted in the ultimate improvement of society even at the expense of personal profit or gain.
9. See for example, the work of Harrod and Skidelsky.
10. See for example, the work of Emmett and Dewey.
11. Knight met his wife, Minerva, while both were students at Milligan.
12. The professor in question, James Edwin Creighton, was Knight's supervisor in the philosophy department.
13. As discussed above, this pluralism reveals itself in his desire to reconcile the subjective characteristics of reality with its objective characteristics.
14. Knight believed that society had evolved in response to unpredictable events and new ideas, but that these changes do not replace the old ways of doing things, but merely alter them.

3. Probability and uncertainty to Knight and to Keynes

It is a world of change in which we live, and a world of uncertainty. We live only by knowing something about the future; while the problems of life, or of conduct at least, arise from the fact that we know so little ...
Frank H. Knight (1921)

It would be foolish, in forming our expectations to attach great importance to matters which are very uncertain.
John M. Keynes (1936)

A study of uncertainty as the ethical basis of Keynes' and Knight's economics must presumably include some consideration of the fundamental similarities and differences that exist between their respective theories. Such a study, however, merely serves to provide insight into the 'economics' of Keynes and Knight, not their 'ethics'. To begin, nonetheless, it is appropriate to develop a clear idea of how their uncertainty theories are similar, how they are different, and more importantly, how they are an integral part of each economist's work. Using the results of such a survey, it will then be possible to explore the deeper *ethics* of Keynes and Knight.

Despite the widespread recognition that both Knight and Keynes focused much of their respective efforts on the role played by uncertainty in economic theory, there has been little discussion of the two in relation to one another. This omission can best be blamed upon the widely-accepted proposition among orthodox economists that uncertainty plays a minimal role in the decisions of economic agents, since rational, utility-maximizing individuals are capable of virtually eliminating uncertainty with the historical information at hand.

Among the occasional research exploring uncertainty that has appeared is a recent collection of articles that discusses uncertainty in economics, including the work of Knight and Keynes.[1] While portions of the book discuss Keynes and Knight in relation to one another, one essay by Maurice Netter suggests that, for the most part, it is inappropriate to discuss one in terms of the other, especially if one is attempting to 'integrate' the two. According to Netter there are simply too many fundamental differences (Netter 1993, 119). Given Knight's and Keynes' divergent views of reality (to be discussed in the following sections), no effort at such integration is to be attempted here. What is abundantly clear, however, is that both economists place uncertainty squarely at the heart of their economics. This fact provides the basis for the study at hand.

Despite his claim that such discussion is inappropriate, Netter nonetheless provides a comprehensive comparison of the uncertainty theories of Knight and Keynes. Accepting Davidson's conclusion that the most fundamental component of the 'Keynesian Revolution' is a very exact and specific notion of uncertainty and the future,[2] he goes on to point out that, even though both Knight and Keynes clearly emphasized uncertainty and its impact upon future expectations, they nonetheless based their understanding of uncertainty on their knowledge of probability. Netter writes, 'Knight and Keynes gave great importance to expectations and their uncertainty. This led them both to situate their understanding of the latter in relation to their understanding of probability ... ' (Netter 1993,112).

As has already been suggested in Chapter 2, the turn of the century was witness to a struggle between religion and science over knowledge and truth. Keynes' emergence from a world of academic and intellectual inquiry directed him toward agreement with those who presumed that probability is a type of knowledge, based upon available information, rather than an object of knowledge. This subjective view[3] stood in contrast to those who suggested that probability was actually a part of external reality, an inherent component of the material world. Knight, and later the supporters of the rational expectations hypothesis[4] adopted this latter view (Lawson 1988, 40).

Despite differences of perspective, it is abundantly clear that Keynes' and Knight's ideas regarding uncertainty are firmly rooted within their conceptions of probability, which are in turn rooted in their opinions regarding external reality. Ultimately, the important point of divergence between Knight and Keynes is less in their probability or uncertainty theories, and more in their respective views of the workings of the real world. Their views regarding external reality become clearer, however, upon examination of their probability theories. Because of this fact, the purpose of this book will best be served by beginning with an examination of Keynes' and Knight's respective understandings about probability before proceeding on to consider each economist's definition and understanding of uncertainty itself.

PROBABILITY TO KEYNES

No discussion of Keynes' work with probability can begin without some reference to the controversy over how Keynes could have published *A Treatise on Probability*[5] in 1921 and then, fifteen years later, have published *The General Theory of Employment, Interest, and Money*. Some argue[6] that there is a more or less direct line of development between Keynes' *Treatise on Probability* and Keynes of the 1930s. Others[7] suggest there is a rather significant change in direction in the development of his thinking and use of probability. Still others[8] reconcile Keynes' changing views on probability as an 'evolution' of thinking, rather than a dramatic 'break' in thought.

In his *A Treatise on Probability* Keynes broaches the subject of uncertainty generally and probability specifically. He contends

> ... the terms *certain* and *probable* describe the various degrees of rational belief about a proposition which different amounts of knowledge authorise us to entertain. All propositions are true or false, but the knowledge we have of them depends on our circumstances; and while it is often convenient to speak of propositions as certain or probable, this expresses strictly a relationship in which they stand to a *corpus* of knowledge, actual or hypothetical, and not a characteristic of the propositions in themselves. (Keynes 1921, 3–4)

Keynes speaks of the subjectivity of probability judgements, the belief that a degree of certainty or probability is contingent upon the knowledge or experience of an individual making the judgement, not upon some innate characteristic of the situation being considered. He continues: 'to this extent, therefore, probability may be called subjective' (Keynes 1921, 4). Of critical importance in reaching the correct understanding of the context of Keynes' statement is proper emphasis upon the words 'to this extent'. Keynes believed, at this point in his thinking, that probability judgements could be called subjective to the extent that people possess different information.

He is quick, however, to point out that probability, as it relates to logic, is *not* subjective. A true probability is not a matter of individual *opinion*. Rather, it is governed by known facts. To Keynes, probability describes a logical relationship between an event and its likelihood of occurring. This relationship is determined by an individual's *accurate* and *correct* degree of belief that some outcome will occur, given the information possessed by the individual (Bateman 1987, 101). It was Keynes' opinion that

> ... a proposition is not probable because we think it so. When once the facts are given which determine our knowledge, what is probable or improbable in these circumstances has been fixed objectively, and is independent of our opinion. The Theory of Probability ... is concerned with the degree of belief which it is

rational to entertain in given conditions, and not merely with the actual beliefs
of particular individuals, which may or may not be rational. (Keynes 1921, 4)

The concession made by Keynes that 'actual beliefs of particular
individuals' might be subject to irrationality provided a point of weakness in
his theory that resulted in criticisms that eventually caused Keynes to rethink
his position. A well-known essay by Keynes' good friend, Frank Ramsey,
published in 1931,[9] finally brought about a public response from Keynes
regarding questions and critiques that had been put forth for a number of
years. Ramsey contended that the beliefs of individuals are not related in
some objective way to various possible outcomes, as Keynes had argued.
Rather, individuals facing uncertainty determine the likelihood of various
possible outcomes and these likelihoods are based upon differing subjective
degrees of belief (Bateman 1987, 106).

Keynes agreed with Ramsey and ultimately conceded that individuals do,
in fact, arrive at the probabilities of expected outcomes at least partially
through subjective interpretation. Still, Keynes maintained that subjectively-
determined expected outcomes do not necessarily mean *rationality*.
Individuals arrive at *rational* decisions only when they correctly and
accurately interpret the available information. It takes more than consistency
in decision making as Ramsey argued, to conclude rational decision making
is taking place (Bateman 1987, 108).

In his *Treatise on Probability*, Keynes had made a distinction between
belief that is rational and belief that is irrational. He wrote

> if a man believes something for a reason which is preposterous or for no reason
> at all, and what he believes turns out to be true for some reason not known to
> him, he cannot be said to believe it *rationally*, although he believes it and it is
> in fact true. On the other hand, a man may rationally believe a proposition to be
> *probable*, when it is in fact false. The distinction between rational belief and
> mere belief, therefore, is not the same as the distinction between true beliefs
> and false beliefs. (Keynes 1921, 10)

Rationality, to Keynes, can only be the result of legitimate, reasonable
information. Even belief in some question that ultimately turns out to be true
cannot be considered *rational* if, in fact, the question might be considered
absurd or 'preposterous'. Likewise, acceptance of a falsehood can be
considered *rational* if the belief is based upon accurate interpretation of
reasonable information.

Probability is therefore related to knowledge via the question of rationality.
Keynes believed that

the highest degree of rational belief, which is termed *certain* rational belief, corresponds to *knowledge*. We may be said to know a thing when we have a certain rational belief in it, and *vice versa*. For reasons which will appear from our account of probable degrees of rational belief … it is preferable to regard *knowledge* as fundamental and to define *rational belief* by reference to it. (Keynes 1921, 10)

Keynes' eventual conclusion, as seen in his later writings, is that probability is not an objective property of reality, but rather one aspect of the way we perceive reality to be (Lawson 1988, 42). Keynes' own perception of reality was that of a non-ergodic, transmutable world possessing a 'permanently uncertain future' (Davidson 1996, 493). Given the existence of such an economic reality, probability analysis becomes applicable only to the most routine and repeatable of events. Keynes believed that 'uncertainty' prevails in all other cases due to the 'characteristic of human nature that a large proportion of our positive activities depend on spontaneous optimism rather than on a mathematical expectation' (Keynes 1936, 161).

The future outcome of most actions taken by individuals or businesses is not usually predictable through the mechanism of probability analysis because 'the full consequences … can only be taken as a result of animal spirits – of a spontaneous urge to action rather than inaction, and not as the outcome of a weighted average of quantitative benefits multiplied by quantitative probabilities' and 'if the animal spirits are dimmed and the spontaneous optimism falters, leaving us to depend on nothing but a mathematical expectation, enterprise will fade and die' (Keynes 1936, 161–2). According to Keynes, this may be the case even if there is no greater likelihood of loss than there is of gain, leaving the application of probability analysis to be of little value in crucial economic decisions.

PROBABILITY TO KNIGHT

Knight's most widely-recognized contribution to the field of economics lies within his distinction between risk and uncertainty, a distinction based upon his application of probability theory. His ideas regarding uncertainty, like those of Keynes, stem from his understanding of probability. According to Knight, probability is largely based upon the judgement of the individual regarding the 'numerical proportion' of some outcome. For Knight, 'this is done by ascertaining the numerical proportion of the cases in which X is associated with Y – which yields the familiar probability judgement. If, say, ninety per cent of X is Y – i.e., if that fraction of objects characterized by property X shows also property Y – the fact may obviously have much the same significance for conduct as if the association were universal' (Knight 1921a, 212).

Knight believed a probability calculation could be applied to situations of unknown or uncertain outcome, as long as one could reasonably know the 'numerical probability' of the outcome. He contended that

> ... even if the proportion is not approximately one hundred per cent, even if it is only half or less, the same fact may hold good. If in a certain class of cases a given outcome is not certain, nor even extremely probable, but only contingent, but if the numerical probability of its occurrence is known, conduct in relation to the situation in question may be ordered intelligently. (Knight 1921a, 213)

Knight therefore suggests that rational individuals are able to make 'intelligent' decisions based upon the 'knowledge' of a numerical probability. Knight identifies the existence of three different ways of determining a 'probability judgement'. The first, *a priori* calculation, applies to simple games of chance, such as the rolling of a fair die. In this case, the possible outcomes are known and the likelihood of a given outcome is equal to the likelihood of another. Knight explains that the first type of judgement is a type of probability almost never encountered in the business world, observing that decisions ordinarily made under conditions of uncertainty might often result in a virtually unlimited number of possible outcomes (Knight 1921a, 224).

The second type of probability judgement, which Knight calls 'statistical', applies to cases in which the possible outcomes are not necessarily known, but are empirically identifiable. This type of situation, unlike the *a priori* judgement, is frequently encountered in business and in life. In this instance, possible outcomes can be identified, based upon 'empirical classification of instances'. Once possible outcomes have been characterized, their likelihood of occurrence can be empirically calculated based upon history. Knight contended, nonetheless, that it must be that 'any high degree of confidence that the proportions found in the past will hold in the future is still based on an *a priori* judgement of indeterminateness' (Knight 1921a, 225). The extent of one's judgement regarding the likelihood of the future being like the past therefore affects the resulting probability calculation.

The final type of probability situation Knight calls an 'estimate'. In this instance, it is impossible to identify all possible outcomes or to calculate the likelihood of their occurrence, but an estimate can nonetheless be reached through the use of statistical application to 'possible' outcomes. 'The distinction is that there is *no valid basis of any kind* for classifying instances' (Knight 1921a, 225). Much of Knight's subsequent attention is directed toward this third type of probability situation.

Knight is critical of theories that propose probability to be based upon our 'ignorance' alone, but he acknowledges that they are widely accepted. He points out 'the fundamental fact underlying probability reasoning is *generally assumed* to be our ignorance' (Knight 1921a, 218), what economic agents do not know, rather than what they do. He asserts that, ' ... the doctrine of real probability, if it is to be valid, must, it seems, rest upon inherent unknowability in the factors, not merely the fact of ignorance' (Knight 1921a, 219). The external reality faced by economic decision makers must therefore be characterized by probability relations inherent in reality but not always knowable to the decision makers themselves.

Knight saw probability, therefore, as being largely determined by the knowledge, or lack of knowledge, possessed by individual decision makers (Knight 1921a, 219). Knight observed that business decisions typically fall into this category of estimation. According to Knight, 'the business man himself not merely forms the best estimate he can of the outcome of his actions, but he is likely also to estimate the probability that his estimate is correct' (Knight 1921a, 226). This *estimate of an estimate* requires both the identification of possible outcomes and the determination of their likelihood of occurrence. These estimates cannot be based upon past experience or history, because of their uniqueness of occurrence. For Knight, 'the essential and outstanding fact is that the 'instance' in question is so entirely unique that there are no others or not a sufficient number to make it possible to tabulate enough like it to form a basis for any inference of value about any real probability in the case we are interested in' (Knight 1921a, 226). Instead, they must be based upon an individual decision maker's best guess. Still, if it is possible to 'know' all factors, either in fact, or in estimation, then probability becomes certainty.

While Knight regards probability as based upon the knowledge possessed by individual economic agents, he nonetheless believes probability to exist as an aspect of material reality itself, part of a deterministic, ergodic 'cosmos'. Knight contends that ' ... the postulates of knowledge generally involve the conclusion that it is really determined in the nature of things which house will burn, which man will die, and which face of the thrown die will come uppermost ... we assume some determinable cause at work; and the results of experience on the whole justify this assumption ... ' (Knight 1921a, 219).

It is this view of a predetermined, predictable, ergodic reality that leads Knight to be more accepting of the classical paradigm than Keynes. Within a largely deterministic world, probability analysis is far more applicable in projecting future outcomes based upon past history. As will be seen, however, Knight's criticisms toward growing income inequality and poverty eventually overwhelm his support for *laissez-faire* and lead him to become critical of a capitalist economy based solely upon such a philosophy, suggesting that individuals typically do not have the prerequisite rationality or intelligence required to face uncertainty, even if the tools to do so are at their disposal.

Keynes differs from Knight primarily in that it is Keynes' suggestion that probability exists as a result of the way in which we understand external reality. For Keynes, a probability calculation is not the result of some objective characteristic of external reality, but rather of how we conceive that reality to be. Even though Keynes clearly believed in a 'probability relationship' that was 'governed by known facts', he conceded that different individuals might arrive subjectively at different probability estimates upon the basis of the information available to them. Knight, on the other hand, suggests that probability exists as a factual characteristic of material reality, but that the accuracy of a probability calculation results from the degree to which economic agents possess information (or knowledge) about the situation in question.

Having developed a general understanding of both Keynes' and Knight's theories of *probability*, including their respective definitions of the concept, it now becomes possible to consider their respective views about *uncertainty*. Uncertainty, to both economists, represented in one form or another a very specific type of probability condition.

UNCERTAINTY TO KEYNES

Despite there being a link between probability and uncertainty, Keynes points out that 'by "very uncertain" I do not mean the same thing as "very improbable"' (Keynes 1936, 148). Rather, Keynes believed uncertainty to exist when there was no basis whatsoever upon which to perform a probability analysis (Keynes, 1937a, 114). Keynes therefore questioned the logic of orthodox, classical economists in basing their theories of efficient, free markets upon the rationality and perfect knowledge of economic agents.

In analyzing Keynes' criticisms of classical economic theory, it is important to understand the basis of the above-mentioned criticisms. Specifically, Keynes' inability to accept classical theory is based upon his observation that mainstream orthodox theories failed to explain the long periods of high unemployment that could be observed during the early part of the twentieth century, especially into the 1920s and 1930s. Keynes believed this unemployment to be caused primarily by insufficient effective demand, brought about by the tendency for economic agents to hold money balances as a hedge against an uncertain future. Despite the wide acceptance of economic models based upon statistical analysis, Keynes did not believe it logical or rational to calculate away uncertainty by applying historical data to questions requiring judgements about the future (Keynes 1936, 148).

Uncertainty has therefore become regarded by many as the most fundamental element of the 'Keynesian revolution'.[10] In particular, Keynes pointed out that uncertainty is evident in the decisions economic agents make regarding whether to hold money balances. This 'liquidity preference' is apparent only under conditions in which money is more than a neutral medium of exchange. If money balances come to be held for 'investment' purposes, or as a 'hedge' against future uncertainty, it becomes obvious that certain necessary conditions under which classical economic theories must be applied do not exist.

Keynes wrote, 'it would be foolish, in forming our expectations, to attach great weight to matters which are very uncertain'. Instead, Keynes believed that individuals base their decisions upon 'facts about which we feel somewhat confident, even though they may be less decisively relevant to the issue than other facts about which our knowledge is vague and scanty' (Keynes 1936, 148). He observed that the tendency for individuals to place great importance upon the observable facts of the past and present heavily influence future expectations, noting that 'the facts of the existing situation enter, in a sense disproportionately, into the formation of our long-term expectations; our usual practice being to take the existing situation and to project it into the future, modified only to the extent that we have more or less definite reasons for expecting a change' (Keynes 1936, 148). In Keynes' world of dynamic, non-ergodic change, the confidence of economic agents is shaken by unpredictability, causing future expectations to depend 'on the *confidence* with which we make this forecast – on how highly we rate the likelihood of our best forecast turning out quite wrong' (Keynes 1936, 148).

Economic agents, to Keynes, simply do not have complete and perfect knowledge about the future, a fact seemingly ignored by those economists steeped in the classical tradition. The impact this revelation has upon decision making is of radical importance. Of special interest to Keynes was the sort of decision made regarding investments and money. In formulating decisions about future yields on investments, agents must consider whether it might be better to hold cash balances or to reduce liquidity by making alternative investments. The knowledge upon which economic agents make these sorts of decisions is often quite limited. Keynes noted:

> The outstanding fact is the extreme precariousness of the basis of knowledge on which our estimates of prospective yield have to be made. Our knowledge of the factors which will govern the yield of an investment some years hence is usually very slight and often negligible. If we speak frankly, we have to admit

that our basis of knowledge for estimating the yield ten years hence of a railway, a copper mine, a textile factory, the goodwill of a patent medicine, an Atlantic liner, the building in the City of London amounts to little and sometimes to nothing; or even five years hence. In fact, those who seriously attempt to make any such estimate are often so much in the minority that their behaviour does not govern the market. (Keynes 1936, 149–50)

Keynes, therefore, questioned the viability of an economy built upon the precepts of classical economics. If perfect and certain knowledge does not or cannot exist, then it becomes impossible for decision makers to account for all possible outcomes or accurately to determine their likelihood of occurrence. Given this observation, individuals might prefer to hold cash balances instead of investing in assets that would otherwise be expected to bring a higher rate of return.

If cash balances are held, a fundamental tenet of classical economic theory is broken. The holding of cash balances is contrary to Say's Law, which suggests that 'supply creates its own demand'. In other words, the production of goods or services creates sufficient incomes to purchase all of the output produced. Under Say's Law, there is never insufficient aggregate demand and there is never any need to hold cash balances. Cash merely serves as a neutral medium of exchange, allowing an individual to exchange one commodity for another without the inconvenience of barter. Keynes explains:

> ... given that the rate of interest is never negative, why should anyone prefer to hold his wealth in a form which yields little or no interest to holding it in a form which yields interest? There is ... a necessary condition failing which the existence of a liquidity-preference for money as a means of holding wealth could not exist. This necessary condition is the existence of *uncertainty* as to the future of the rate of interest, *i.e.* as to the complex rates of interest for varying maturities which will rule at future dates. (Keynes 1936, 168)

If uncertainty did not exist, it would make no sense for individuals to hold money balances. There would be no fear of losing the value of one's wealth if that wealth were invested in some longer-term, interest bearing investment. Only if the possibility exists that wealth could be lost, does it make sense to choose cash as an investment alternative. According to Keynes,

> thus if a need for liquid cash may conceivably arise ... there is a risk of a loss being incurred in purchasing a long-term debt and subsequently turning it into cash, as compared to holding cash. The actuarial profit or mathematical expectation of gain calculated in accordance with the existing probabilities – if it can be calculated, which is doubtful – must be sufficient to compensate for the risk of disappointment. (Keynes 1936, 169)

Neoclassical interpretations notwithstanding, it is perhaps correct, therefore, to observe that the 'Keynesian Revolution' can be characterized by its focus upon what Netter and others refer to as 'radical uncertainty' (Netter 1993, 112) or the impossibility of determining the future accurately on the basis of the statistical history of the past. While many modern economists have identified the issue of uncertainty as the foundational basis for Keynes' break from classical economic theory, this is far from universal. The school of thought espousing a 'neoclassical synthesis', for example, recognized the superficial differences between the economics of Keynes and the economics of those who came before him. They did not, however, recognize that the most fundamental difference of all was Keynes' placement of uncertainty at the heart of his work.

UNCERTAINTY TO KNIGHT

While Keynes rejected the classical economic model because of the untenability of its underlying axioms, Frank Knight, by contrast, allowed the classical model to remain as the accepted paradigm within his own economic theories. Furthermore, while Keynes left room for debate regarding his emphasis upon uncertainty, Knight left no such room for doubt about how much importance should be placed upon uncertainty in his economics. He gained widespread recognition, but not universal acceptance, for his placement of uncertainty at the core of his classically-oriented economic theories.

Rather than uncertainty bringing about criticism of capitalism, as had been the case in the work of Keynes, Knight came to endorse a system of *laissez-faire* partly *because* of uncertainty. Specifically, Knight suggested that profit is the result of effective decision making in the face of uncertainty. Uncertainty, Knight would say, is a characteristic of *actual* competition, not *perfect* competition. As such, including uncertainty in one's economic model provides for a more realistic, and therefore accurate, understanding of economic behavior.

Knight was specific in his distinction between risk on the one hand, and uncertainty on the other. For Knight, the term 'uncertainty' refers to situations requiring that decisions be made based upon non-quantifiable factors, while 'risk' refers to a '*measurable* uncertainty' (Knight 1921a, 20). In distinguishing between risk and uncertainty, Knight wrote that

> ... the practical difference between the two categories, risk and uncertainty, is that in the former the distribution of the outcome in a group of instances is known (either through calculation *a priori* or from statistics of past

experience), while in the case of uncertainty this is not true, the reason being in general that it is impossible to form a group of instances, because the situation dealt with is in a high degree unique. (Knight 1921a, 233)

Uncertainty is the result in the event of such unique occurrences, preventing the application of statistical analysis and leaving decision makers no choice but to 'make a guess' about the future outcome.

Much of Knight's *Risk, Uncertainty, and Profit* was devoted to recapitulating the classical model of a competitive market economy. Knight was, nonetheless, skeptical of whether economic agents possessed the degree of rationality assumed by the neoclassical, Marshallian economists upon whose theories Knight built his own. Still, he accepted the necessity of many of their simplifying assumptions, given the impossibility of recreating the controlled laboratory conditions enjoyed by the physical sciences. To Knight, it was necessary to simplify the features of the real world, as the neoclassical economists had done, in order to 'show the operation of the forces at work free from all disturbing influences' (Knight 1921a, 197).

Knight recognized with some incredulity the assumption of perfect and complete knowledge on the part of economic agents. He claimed that 'chief among the simplifications of reality prerequisite to the achievement of perfect competition is, as has been emphasized all along, the assumption of practical omniscience on the part of every member of the competitive system' (Knight 1921a, 197). Knight did not accept the notion of 'practical omniscience' and devoted much of his effort toward explaining why profit is, in fact, the result of this lack of perfect knowledge.

Knight accepted the concept that, assuming perfect competition, long-run economic profits would be nonexistent, competed away by the actions of the numerous entrepreneurs. In Knight's model, entrepreneurs were all negotiating for the purchase of productive resources in order to bring their product to market, which would be sold at a price arrived at by competitive forces as well. This led Knight to the conclusion that all of these activities were conducted on the basis of 'anticipation' of resource and product selling prices (Knight 1921a, 198). It was because these 'anticipations' sometimes prove incorrect that in the short run, profits arise for some, losses for others.

Knight blamed imperfect knowledge in the face of a changing world for the incorrect future predictions of economic agents. He observed: 'it is a world of change in which we live, and a world of uncertainty. We live only by knowing *something* about the future; while the problems of life, or of conduct at least, arise from the fact that we know so little. This is as true of business as of other spheres of activity' (Knight 1921a, 199). For Knight, it is the presence of imperfect or incomplete knowledge regarding *change* that gives rise to profit and loss. He continued, if all changes were to take place in accordance with invariable and universally known laws, they could be foreseen for an indefinite period in advance of their occurrence, and would not upset the perfect apportionment of product values among the contributing agencies, and profit (or loss) would not arise. Hence, it is our imperfect knowledge of the future, a consequence of change, not change as such, which is crucial for the understanding of our problem. (Knight 1921a, 198)

Knight was specific in his analysis that it is not an absence of knowledge that is the issue. Rather, it is the degree of knowledge possessed that is in question. It was Knight's contention that economic decisions are made based upon the degree of information and knowledge available. This knowledge is utilized by the decision maker to form an *opinion* upon which decisions are based. 'The essence of the situation is action according to *opinion*, of greater or less foundation and value, neither entire ignorance nor complete and perfect information, but partial knowledge' (Knight 1921a, 199).

Actions based upon this partial knowledge, according to Knight, result in the disappointment of expectations, bringing about the failure of the economic system to arrive at the desired allocation of resources and an equitable distribution of income. For Knight, a fundamental flaw in the construct of rational economic agents was the notion that knowledge presumes the existence of '*things*, which, *under the same circumstances, always behave in the same way*' (Knight 1921a, 204). Knight observed that not only was it virtually impossible to identify all '*things*', but it was equally impossible to identify all '*circumstances*'.

Knight, nonetheless, proceeds to construct a model in which intelligent, if not rational, decisions can be made. He accomplishes this by aggregation. That is, he suggests that individuals do not make decisions about the future based upon *things*, but about *kinds of things*. He states: 'it must be possible not merely to assume that the *same* thing will always behave in the same way, but that the *same kind* of thing will do the same, and that there is in fact a finite, practically manageable number of *kinds* of things' (Knight 1921a, 205). For Knight, finite intelligence made it necessary for there be some constancy in the number and type of 'groupings' that could be observed. Knight therefore differs from Keynes in that Knight considers the world to be ergodic and therefore predictable, given the power of 'aggregation'.

Knight's recognition that agents do not possess perfect knowledge led him to enter philosophical ground. He wrote: 'If we are to understand the workings of the economic system we must examine the meaning and significance of uncertainty; and to this end some inquiry into the nature and function of knowledge itself is necessary' (Knight 1921a, 199). Despite the existence of a deterministic, ergodic world, Knight believed the lack of perfect and complete knowledge among economic agents prevented them from accurately predicting the results of future events in every case. The power of aggregation was not applicable to the case of a 'higher form of uncertainty not susceptible to measurement and hence to elimination. It is this *true uncertainty* which by preventing the theoretically perfect outworking of the tendencies of competition gives the characteristic form of "enterprise" to economic organizations as a whole and accounts for the peculiar income of the entrepreneur' (Knight 1921a, 232).

THE SIGNIFICANT DIFFERENCES

The preceding discussion has revealed that it is accurate to conclude that both Knight and Keynes maintained similar ideas about uncertainty itself, based upon the impossibility of determining the accurate probability distributions of certain events. It is inaccurate to conclude, however, despite similar definitions, that they meant the same thing. When Knight and Keynes each claimed that uncertainty is the result of immeasurable probability, they each had something very different in mind. For Knight, economic agents lack the knowledge or the intelligence to arrive at accurate estimates of otherwise ergodic probabilities. For Keynes, such estimates simply do not exist in a non-ergodic world (see Davidson 1996).

The essential difference to be made between Knight and Keynes is therefore less in their views about uncertainty and more in their respective views of reality as manifested in their conceptions of probability. By accepting the classical economic model, Knight also accepts the notion of an immutable, ergodic reality in which economic agents are able, given the requisite rationality and intellect, to accurately predict the outcome of future events. Keynes, on the other hand, rejects the axiom of ergodicity, recognizing that economic agents often know that they are dealing with a non-ergodic, unpredictable world and behave accordingly.

The extent to which the theological and intellectual influences upon Knight and Keynes affected their conception of probability and uncertainty is perhaps arguable. What is certain, based upon the evidence at hand, is that both Knight's and Keynes' world views were affected to *some* extent by the formative influences discussed in Chapter 2. Keynes' emergence from a rational, logical, intellectual environment of enlightened thinking instilled in him a faith in man's ability to affect his destiny despite being faced by a non-ergodic world. The conservative, theologically-based education of Knight's early years created a skeptical cynicism in Knight, leaving him to believe that man was at the mercy of a predetermined 'cosmos' and that man himself lacked sufficient intelligence to effectively face the uncertainty of a changing, dynamic world.

Keynes made a distinction between probability and uncertainty when he said 'by "very uncertain" I do not mean the same thing as "very improbable"' (Keynes 1936, 148). Uncertainty to Keynes was based upon what Perlman and McCann call 'fragility' (Perlman *et al.* 1993, 13) and what Davidson calls a 'nonprobabilistic creative economic external reality' (Davidson 1996, 493). Decision makers are simply unable to foretell the future. For a proposition to be *improbable* suggests that it remains possible to measure its 'unlikelihood' of occurring, despite belief that its unlikelihood is very great. For a proposition to be *uncertain* suggests that we remain unable to determine with a high degree of confidence what the future will bring.

Knight likewise separated risk from uncertainty by pointing out that risk is quantifiable through the use of probability calculus. Uncertainty exists when it remains impossible to determine or assign probabilities to an event's likelihood of occurrence. This impossibility of numerical calculation rests within the inherent uniqueness of events. Given the possibility that events are in many ways unique from all other events, it may prove impossible to compare the expected future with the known past. Nonetheless, Knight left room for events to be 'grouped' with other similar events. It might then be possible to assign numerical probabilities to these larger groupings since it may then be within our intellectual power to do so. A smaller number of grouped events each possessing a broader range of characteristics is more comparable to other similar groupings since there are (1) few items to compare and (2) a larger number of characteristics in common with one another.

Lawson[11] has attempted to provide a classification illustrating the significant differences between the respective theories of uncertainty and probability to Keynes, Knight, the followers of the rational expectations[12] hypothesis, as well as Savage and Friedman.[13] His four – quadrant table shows uncertainty as being numerically measurable probability and uncertainty as being numerically immeasurable probability intersecting with probability as both a *property* of knowledge and an *object* of knowledge as a property of external material reality (Lawson 1988, 48). His classification system of both probability and uncertainty theories is reproduced as Table 3.1.

Lawson's table suggests that Keynes adopted a theory of uncertainty in which probability is a property of knowledge or belief and uncertainty corresponds to a situation of numerically immeasurable probability (Lawson 1988, 48). Knight, on the other hand, falls into the quadrant in which probability theory, at least as it pertains to the type of probability 'estimates' seen in business, is an object of knowledge as a property of external material

Table 3.1 *Lawson's 'Initial schematic classification of prominent accounts of probability and uncertainty in economic analysis'*

	Probability is a property of knowledge or belief	Probability is also an object of knowledge as a property of external material reality
Uncertainty corresponds to a situation of numerical	*Subjectivists (e.g., Savage, Friedman)*	*Proponents of the rational expectations view*
Uncertainty corresponds to a situation of numerically *im*measurable probability	*Keynes*	*Knight*

reality. Uncertainty for Knight, as with Keynes, corresponds to a situation of numerically immeasurable probability (Lawson 1988, 48).

It remains to be seen whether these differences in theory have any impact upon the ultimate policy recommendations of Keynes and Knight. Still, given their respective understandings of probability as seen in their views of 'reality', it can be observed that both economists maintained very different world views. As will be seen, these contrasting world views lead to very different economic outlooks and policy recommendations

Knight adopts the view that mankind is at the mercy of a predetermined, and ultimately predictable, natural order. Economic actors are relatively powerless to take actions that will improve their long-term[14] state of being, since to do so impedes the working of the free forces of the market. Keynes, on the other hand, is of the opinion that it is perhaps not in man's best interest simply to allow the economic world to spin undisturbed. It is, rather, in the best interest of society and, in turn, of individual members of society, for them to take action on their own to correct for the economic system's imperfections. The question of Keynes' and Knight's economics becomes a question of free will against predestination, of one's ability to determine one's own future against inevitable and unchangeable results.

NOTES

1. *Uncertainty in Economic Thought* – edited by Schmidt (1993).
2. According to Davidson, 'the economic system is moving through calendar time from an irrevocable past to an uncertain and statistically unpredictable future. Past and present

market data do not necessarily provide correct signals regarding future outcomes. This means, in the language of statistics, that economic data are not necessarily generated by a stochastic ergodic process' (Davidson 1994, 17).

3. As will be discussed in the following section, Keynes initially believed probabilities to be the result of objectively known facts. Keynes recognized, however, the subjectivity of people's opinions about the likelihood of an event occurring, leading him to believe in the subjectivity of a given individual's probability analysis and to conclude that such subjectivity made the application of probability analysis to matters of economics less useful.

4. The Rational Expectations Hypothesis, introduced by Robert Lucas, was an articulation of Milton Friedman's 'fooling model'. Lucas suggested that expectations are rational when individuals make decisions based upon the available information, including past mistakes.

5. *A Treatise on Probability*, while published widely in 1921, was an elaboration of his Cambridge thesis, dated 1916.

6. For example, O'Donnell, Carabelli, and Skidelsky.

7. For example, Wittgenstein, Ramsey, and Davis.

8. Including Bradley Bateman (1987).

9. The essay, 'Truth and Probability' was written in 1926. Ramsey was a contemporary of Keynes, a fellow Apostle, and had been born and raised at Cambridge.

10. Including, among others, Weintraub (1975) and Davidson (1992, 1994).

11. Tony Lawson (1988).

12. In the rational expectations models, the agent is assumed to already know the correct short-run estimate of the long-run objective probability distribution, i.e., the subjective probability distribution equals the objective probability distribution.

13. Subjectivists, including Friedman and Savage, regard probability to be the 'degree of belief in a given proposition or event, held by an actual individual at some specific point in time' (Lawson 1988, 40–41). Despite the use of probability analysis by subjectivists, they claim that an individual's 'knowledge' of a given probability distribution does not necessarily mean it is, in fact, a reflection of reality.

14. Knight recognized, however, the existence of short-run profits, produced by entrepreneurs able to accurately predict an uncertain, short-run future.

4. The ethical implications of uncertainty to Knight and to Keynes

*If there is a real indeterminateness,
and if the ultimate seat of it is in the activities of the human machine, there is
in a sense an opening of the door to a conception of freedom and conduct ...*
Frank H. Knight (1921)

*Many of the greatest economic evils of our time are the fruits of risk,
uncertainty, and ignorance.*
John M. Keynes (1926)

With a reasonably concise understanding of the meaning of uncertainty to Keynes and to Knight achieved, the question of ethics may now be addressed more directly. The placement of uncertainty at the core of both economists' economic theories must not be examined as merely a question of mechanics. Rather, given the 'economist as philosopher' categorization of both men, a more comprehensive examination must include consideration of the ethical implications of uncertainty in their work.

The identification of uncertainty as an endogenous component of economic reality, and the recognition that its existence has a significant influence upon economic decision making, is evidence that both Knight and Keynes went far beyond the traditional use of the generally accepted Benthamite calculus in building their respective understandings of economic behavior. This logical, analytical extension makes it apparent that Knight and Keynes recognized that economic agents do not necessarily possess the perfect and complete knowledge required to make rational, economically sound decisions. The absence of such knowledge forces individuals to make decisions based upon varying degrees of information, which differ from one individual to another. This variation of knowledge means decisions must be made with a high degree of dependence upon the subjective value judgements and opinions of individuals.

Given that Knight and Keynes developed their notions of uncertainty from different theoretical foundations, it should come as no surprise that the role played by uncertainty in the economic analysis of Keynes and Knight takes on somewhat different dimensions and perspectives as well. While the focus of Keynes' concern regarding 'uncertainty' lies in the role it plays in bringing about a 'liquidity preference', resulting in insufficient aggregate demand, Knight's analysis, by contrast, focuses upon the role uncertainty plays in being an 'obstacle' to the accurate prediction of the future. In the analysis of Keynes, the major economic actor is the individual consumer or entrepreneur, who chooses to hold cash balances, postponing consumption or investment until a later, unspecified time period (Keynes 1936, 166). In the analysis of Knight, it is the entrepreneur most able to accurately predict an uncertain future who is deserving of the highest profit as a reward for overcoming such an obstacle (Knight 1921a, 268).

While Knight and Keynes proceeded from somewhat different perspectives, brought about by different backgrounds and influences, both economists shared common ground in the idea that economics was more than a science of efficient resource allocation. They shared common agreement that economics was indeed a 'moral' science, misused by many of their predecessors and contemporaries as a tool in man's search for knowledge. While many economists in the early part of the twentieth century became more and more dependent upon mathematics and statistical (econometric) analysis to bring about what they believed to be greater knowledge, Knight and Keynes clung to the more realistic notion that not everything was 'knowable'. Also, Knight and Keynes go further than many other economists, providing insight into the subtle, yet important differences between the possession of knowledge and the possession of rationality.

Nonetheless, Knight and Keynes went their own ways in elaborating their respective ethical concerns regarding the workings of a free-market, capitalist economy. Specifically, they were especially concerned with the relationship between the individual and the society to which he belonged and whether decisions made by individuals in pursuit of improving their own personal welfare would, in fact, be for the good or detriment of society at large. It is in this context that the role of uncertainty within economic theory takes on an ethical dimension. Accordingly, the degree of political involvement becomes not only an economic question, but also an ethical one, made especially clear in Keynes' criticism of classical economic precepts and Knight's analysis of economic freedom versus economic power.

ECONOMICS AS A MORAL SCIENCE

John Dewey wrote 'conduct as moral may thus be defined as *activity called forth and directed by ideas of value or worth, where the values concerned are so mutually incompatible as to require consideration and selection before an overt action is entered upon*' (Dewey 1908, 209). The moral and ethical question of individual freedom versus social harmony grew more acute during the early part of the twentieth century. The apparent incompatibility of decisions made by self-interested individuals and policies enacted by governments in pursuit of social good meant some reconciliation had to occur in order for capitalism to function as intended.

With freedom for the individual to determine his own actions established as a fundamental precept of capitalism, it became necessary to reconcile the 'rights' of the individual with the 'rights' of the community. As the machine of capitalism evolved, as it was certainly doing in the early part of the twentieth century, the conflict between individual and social action grew more pronounced.[1] The choices made by individuals in pursuit of their own self-interest often came into conflict with the best interest of society as a whole. What was regarded as 'the Gilded Age' by some was also regarded as a 'Tragic Era' by others, characterized by a ' ... puritan, capitalist society, with [a] distorted system of values, emphasis on the useful, [and] hostility to the artist ... ' (Leuchtenburg 1958, 146).

With utilitarianism accepted as the general rule of economic law, however, it remained problematic to suggest that anything other than general acceptance of a system of *laissez-faire* should be considered in directing economic activity. Nevertheless, the acceptance of an orthodox economic theory of *laissez-faire* implies an acceptance of an inherent 'goodness' of man, such that the economic decisions made by individuals are not made at the expense of other members of society. Thus, the questions of economics, dealing with decisions affecting not only individuals but society as well, became recognized as questions rooted in morality and ethics. Both Keynes and Knight recognized early on that the questions of economics must rightly be viewed as possessing a certain dimension of moral and ethical valuation, and saw economics as a channel through which these moral and ethical questions might somehow be resolved.

Keynes observed ' ... I also want to emphasise strongly the point about economics being a moral science ... it deals with introspection and with values ... it deals with motives, expectations, psychological uncertainties' (Keynes 1938b, 300). Additionally, as was previously cited, Keynes recognized that, since capitalism appeals to the 'money-loving instincts' of man, economics must address the issue of monetary motivation as well. This motivation manifests itself most prominently in the attempts by individuals to maximize their lifetime utility and by businesses to maximize profits. As far as Keynes and Knight were concerned, the important questions of 'economic man' do not deal with the mechanics of general equilibrium or constrained optimization, but rather with the ability of economic agents to pursue their own 'money-motives' without unfairly inhibiting other members of society from doing so as well.

The Indeterminancy of Keynes

Keynes has long been recognized for his criticism of *laissez-faire*.[2] While critical of the philosophy of *laissez-faire*, however, he did not extend his criticism directly to the ideology of capitalism itself. Rather, Keynes worked diligently to remedy the problems he believed were inherent in capitalist economies. He even remarked in his 1926 essay, 'The End of *Laissez-Faire*',[3] that

> these reflections have been directed toward possible improvements in the technique of modern capitalism by the agency of collective action ... for my part I think that capitalism, wisely managed, can probably be made more efficient for attaining economic ends than any alternative system yet in sight, but that in itself it is in many ways extremely objectionable. Our problem is to work out a social organization which shall be as efficient as possible without offending our notions of a satisfactory way of life. (Keynes 1926, 292–4).

Rather than promoting some sort of centrally-planned socialist economic order, Keynes finds political legitimacy only insofar as the objectives of the state are limited to increasing the happiness and welfare of the people (Helburn 1992, 29).

This early essay of Keynes reveals his contempt not for capitalism, but for the direction economic theory had evolved in blind support of certain underlying precepts of capitalism. Specifically, he was critical of the notion that individuals possessed the perfect and complete knowledge necessary to accurately perform the calculations required to achieve the most efficient (and socially optimal) allocation of resources possible. Lacking this perfect knowledge, individuals are left to make judgements or 'guesses' regarding the outcome of future events. These judgements are, by definition, based to a very great degree upon values,[4] which are inherently subjective.

Keynes' concerns were based upon his understanding of the historical evolution of *laissez-faire*. He identified three 'currents', through which society had evolved throughout the eighteenth and nineteenth centuries in reaching its present state of preference for *laissez-faire* in regard to public policy. The first current was the acceptance of individualism. Keynes remarks ' ... Locke and Hume ... founded Individualism. The compact [agreement] presumed rights in the individual; the new ethics, being no more than a scientific study of the consequences of rational self-love, placed the individual at the centre'[5] (Keynes 1926, 272–3). Specifically, Keynes lamented the 'new ethics' of Benthamite utility calculations, performed by individuals with an ever-growing preference for pleasure and aversion to pain. Keynes observed that these notions supported the preferences of rational individuals seeking to maximize their lifetime utility by furnishing ' ... a satisfactory intellectual foundation to the rights of property and to the liberty of the individual in possession to do what he liked with himself and with his own' (Keynes 1926, 273).

While Keynes pointed to individualism as an eighteenth century contribution to *laissez-faire*, he recognized that the egalitarian philosophies of the nineteenth century did not conflict with the previous contribution of individualism, but complemented it. It was Keynes' observation that this 'second current' of egalitarianism united with its apparent opposite, individualism, via the efforts of economists. Keynes remarked 'the idea of a divine harmony between private advantage and the public good is already apparent in Paley.[6] But it was the economists who gave the notion a good scientific basis' (Keynes 1926, 274).

It was, in fact, 'the philosophical doctrine that government has no need to interfere ... ' that came to 'harmonise individualism and socialism' (Keynes 1926, 274). It is the mixing of this 'third current' with the previous two that brings economics into the realm of ethics. Keynes makes clear his intention to improve the state of society through improvements to capitalism itself. While the specifics of his recommendations for the improvement of capitalism will be discussed in more detail in Chapter 6, it is appropriate at this juncture to clarify the intent of those recommendations. He goes so far as to say 'these reflections have been directed towards possible improvement in the technique of capitalism by the agency of collective action' (Keynes 1926, 292–3).

Contrary to the philosophy of Bentham, Paley, and Smith, Keynes remained unconvinced that the uncoordinated actions of individuals would always result in outcomes that served the best interests of society as a whole. Keynes reached this highly unorthodox conclusion in part because of his observation that most economic agents were unable to make economically efficient decisions in the presence of uncertainty, despite the claims by classical economists to the contrary.

Nonetheless, Keynes appears ready for the inevitable criticism that his policy recommendations might appear to lean toward the side of 'socialism', offending those who heartily accept the ' ... essential characteristic of capitalism, namely the dependence upon an intense appeal to the money-making and money-loving instincts of individuals as the main motive force of the economic machine' (Keynes 1926, 293). While recognizing the ethical conflict between individualism and egalitarianism, it is the broad-based acceptance of 'money-making' and 'money-loving' that leads Keynes to recognize not only the ethical but also the moral implications of economics. He continues ' ... the fiercest contests and the most deeply felt divisions of opinion are likely to be waged in the coming years not round technical questions ... but round those which, for want of better words, may be called psychological or, perhaps, moral' (Keynes 1926, 293).

The root of this morality question is to be found, according to Keynes, in the fact that there is an 'indeterminancy' within matters of economic decision making that cannot be resolved using the application of statistical techniques based upon past history and present circumstance. Because individual motives, expectations, and opinions vary, economic decisions are not carried out in an entirely objective manner. Rather, the subjectivity of individual opinion enters into virtually all economic decision making (Bateman and Davis 1991, 91).

The Uncertainty of Knight

Widely regarded as a philosopher/economist,[7] Knight points out in a 1929 essay that 'students of ethics or social science hardly need to be reminded that one of the leading modern schools of ethical thought has been dominated by economists. The English-speaking world in particular has been utilitarian in its theory and its folk-mind from the age of the Enlightenment. Hence some reflections by an economist on utilitarianism and ethics generally may be worth consideration' (Knight 1929, 129). Knight understood the ethical implications of economics and especially the ramifications of the existence of uncertainty within the workings of a market-driven economic system.

Knight pointed out ' ... economics and ethics naturally come into rather intimate relations with each other since both recognizedly deal with the problem of value' (Knight 1923, 19). Of special relevance to Knight was the unknowability and unpredictability of human wants. This creates a problem unique to economics as a 'science' since human wants are 'universally and unquestioningly recognized' as fundamental data elements in the work of economists (Knight 1923, 20).

Knight believed that human 'wants' took on characteristics of 'values' or 'oughts' and, as such, were not subject to 'scientific description or logical manipulation' (Knight 1923, 21). Knight recognized that human wants and needs changed and evolved over time and that some wants went unfulfilled while the goods and services of business activity brought fulfillment to others. This inconsistency and predilection for change makes human wants more difficult to classify as scientific variables. As such, Knight contends, human wants cannot be objectively classified and incorporated into mathematical calculations intended to maximize the utility of the individual (Knight 1923, 41). While Knight accepted the prevailing orthodoxy of value, in the sense of exchange being largely determined by utility, he did not accept any suggestion that prices were a reflection of 'value in any truly ethical sense' (Schweikhardt 1988, 409).

Of special concern to Knight throughout his career were the questions of income distribution and whether a capitalist economy characterized by a policy of *laissez-faire* would indeed result in an equitable and fair distribution of income shares. Specifically, Knight extended his analysis of income distribution to include detailed examination of 'utilitarianism' (Knight 1929) and its theoretical basis in individual decision making. His analysis also included the concept of 'economic freedom' (Knight 1929 and 1960), suggesting that government action should be kept at a minimum if individuals were to be empowered to pursue their own self-interest, which Knight, among others, viewed as their right.

The ethical dimension of this issue was seen by Knight to rest in the question of whether decisions made by individuals in pursuit of satisfying their own self-interest would, in fact, be in conformity with the best interest of society as a whole. Knight wrote,

> ... an organized system must operate in accordance with a *social* standard. This standard will of course be related in some way to the values of the individuals making up the society, but it cannot be merely identical with them; it presupposes some process of organizing the various individual interests, weighing them against each other and adjudicating conflicts among them. (Knight 1923, 42)

Thus, the question of 'what is good' became an economic question, with obvious roots in ethics. Knight observed that capitalism had evolved to its present state in part because of the influence of utilitarianism (Knight 1929, 130). What had become generally accepted as 'good' was therefore influenced by utilitarian ethics.

Knight wrote 'the important point, however, is that for utilitarianism good is individual, and the individual is the ultimate judge of it; what is good is that the individual shall get what he wants' (Knight 1929, 130). For a capitalist economy, therefore, it had become customary for individuals to have significant freedoms to direct their own affairs and to make their own economic decisions. In fact, the prevailing view within capitalist economies, and certainly of classical economic thinkers, was that government involvement in the economy should be kept at a minimum so that individual decision making would not be hindered. He continued ' ... the actual goal of political action then became the essentially negative ideal of *freedom*, i.e., the "greatest good" will be realized through "maximum freedom". Details were worked out by the British laissez faire economists, beginning with Bentham's older contemporary, Adam Smith, and culminating in Herbert Spencer[8] ... ' (Knight 1929, 130).

Unlike Adam Smith and his followers, Knight did not build his case for *laissez-faire* upon the argument that individuals are better able than governments to make sound, socially optimal economic decisions because of the governments inability to do so. He stated 'it need not be assumed that the individual's knowledge is perfect, or even very good, but only that it is *better* than that of the outside agency of control, practically speaking a political bureaucracy' (Knight 1929, 130–31). Knight not only recognized the ethical struggle between decision making for the benefit of the individual versus society but also the role played by the knowledge possessed by the individuals involved. He continues 'Smith and his followers notoriously placed their emphasis on the stupidity of governments rather than the competence of individuals, and the modern reader must keep in mind the character of the governments which formed the basis of their judgements' (Knight 1929, 131).

Despite recognizing that uncertainty is 'one of the fundamental facts of life' (Knight 1921a, 347), Knight came to question not only the possibility of reducing uncertainty, but of its distribution as well. Knight considered the ethical implication of uneven distributions of uncertainty among individuals and among firms when he recognized 'the very essence of free enterprise is the concentration of responsibility ... and taking of consequences of decisions ... ' (Knight 1921a, 349). Knight contended that free enterprise was justified on the grounds that ' ... men make decisions, exercise control, more effectively if they are made responsible for the results of the correctness, or the opposite, of those decisions' (Knight 1921a, 358). To Knight, it is the presence of uncertainty that brings about the legitimacy of financial reward (profit) for making correct decisions. Greater socialization of economic decision making would remove the ability of free enterprise to function, given that responsibility for decision making, and the accompanying consequences would no longer be in the hands of individuals.

Economics has, through its varied uses, provided individuals and society with a tool in their search for knowledge, a channel for reconciliation between the possession of knowledge and the possession of rationality, and a path bringing to a common ground the battle between individualist economics and socialism. The corollary issues of economic freedom versus economic power likewise enter into the equation. While Knight and Keynes did not always agree with the ways in which their predecessors or their peers had utilized economics, they did recognize that these facets of the social science placed it squarely within the realm of ethics and morality.

ECONOMICS AS THE MEANS TO OUR SEARCH FOR KNOWLEDGE

G.E. Moore said of knowledge,

> ... whenever we make any assertion whatever (unless we do not mean what we say) we are always *expressing* one or other of two things – namely, either that we *think* the thing in question to be so or that we *know* it to be so ... it may be held, that we always only believe or think that an action is right or wrong, and never really *know* which it is; that, when, therefore, we assert one to be so, we are always merely expressing an opinion or belief, never expressing *knowledge*. (Moore 1903, 125)

Moore's influence upon Keynes has already been identified. Here, the influence is obvious, given Keynes' adoption of the view that in many cases, things simply are unknowable. Knight, too, recognized the inherent 'unknowability' of certain things, as evidenced by his separation of uncertainty and risk.

In Chapter 2 it was noted that by the late 1800s economics had come to replace theology in helping society to govern and direct its actions. Even if one accepts the role played by economics in filling certain voids left by theology, one might question the influence of theology upon the development of economic thought itself. How might a science such as economics, which places so much emphasis upon the maximization of pleasure (utility) and financial gain (profit) have any basis in theology? It is precisely *because* questions of economics are questions of the individual and therefore of society, or perhaps it is the *individual versus society*, that they can be viewed as being theologically–based.

Part of having an accepted framework, an accepted paradigm, is some concept of the fundamental nature of things, such as Dow's previously mentioned ' ... notion of regularity or order'.[9] Questions related to creation and purpose direct the inquisitive to explore for possible answers, with the exploration largely being conducted within generally accepted, paradigm-driven parameters. Theology is, at its core, about the search for knowledge and the search for an elusive truth and has historically provided individuals with a personal and social mechanism through which this search can be carried out.

Since the beginning of recorded history, if not before, people have longed to know and to understand their origins and purpose for being, but in all of this searching, they have met with precious little success. Despite technological advances that have brought great progress to civilization, it would seem we have no greater 'knowledge' about 'truth' than we did when we began our efforts. In the end, knowledge requires belief, which requires faith, and as such, knowledge is largely subjective, albeit based upon objective criteria to one degree or another. As both Knight and Keynes recognized, this subjectivity of knowledge, and thus of truth, is the basis for concluding that ethics is integral to economic thought.

Ontological and epistemological inquiries have long dominated the work of many economists. Such lines of inquiry must have some theological basis, since the ultimate answers to questions of 'truth' and the 'nature of things' must logically include conclusions or at least assumptions about creation itself. Certainly Adam Smith's concepts of human nature and behavior were built upon theological constructs. Influenced by the deist thinking of the Enlightenment era, it is evident that Smith based his economic model upon the notion of individuals in pursuit of 'the end', or real satisfaction of genuine needs, via 'the means', or the deceptive satisfaction of greed-based want. These individuals possess certain 'endowments', which have been bestowed upon them as part of their human nature. Choices are made based not only upon the interest for one's self, but also upon 'sympathy' for others. Clearly, Smith made no distinction between the economic self and the economic community. To Smith, the pursuit of self-interest, tempered with sympathy for others, assured that the good of society was served (Smith 1759, 47). Ultimately, however, this idealistic view of sympathetic economic agents gave way to a view in which self-interest outweighs sympathy and the goals of individuals conflict with those of society.

It is evident that whatever methodology is ultimately accepted by economists is largely based upon their understanding of the prevailing paradigm and the extent to which they have knowledge of it. Keynes' *Treatise on Probability*, largely regarded as highly philosophical in nature, reveals much about his thinking on the matter of 'knowledge' and 'truth'. Despite claiming initially that he is not interested in the exploration of such philosophical issues, he goes on to do just that. Furthermore, Keynes' later work reveals a tendency to be at least as interested in philosophy as he was in economics. Nonetheless, early in his *Treatise on Probability*, Keynes proclaims: 'I do not wish to become involved in questions of epistemology to which I do not know the answer ... but some explanation is necessary if the reader is to be put in a position to understand the point of view from which the author sets out ... ' (Keynes 1921, 10).

A portion of what Keynes sought to do in his *Treatise on Probability* was to make clear his thoughts on 'knowledge', which Keynes took to be at least partially rooted in the mathematics of probability. His concern over certainty and its corollary, uncertainty, is made evident in this early work. Keynes states, ' ... the highest degree of rational belief, which is termed *certain* rational belief, corresponds to *knowledge*' (Keynes 1921, 10). While recognizing the value of probability in the process of individual decision making, Keynes was quick to point out its shortcomings, particularly in the use of probability in the search for 'truth'. He makes the claim: ' ... it has been pointed out already that no knowledge of probabilities, less in degree than certainty, helps us to know what conclusions are true ... '(Keynes 1921, 322–3). Keynes' concept of knowledge is that it is 'incompletable' (Rymes 1994, 141).

Knight states emphatically that while economics is a 'science', it differs from the natural sciences, primarily in the way in which it deals with knowledge and truth. Knight is critical of attempts to generalize economics into the same methodological techniques of the natural sciences. Knight's criticism stems from his belief that the methodology of economics simply does not involve physical observation of facts or reality as do the sciences of chemistry, biology, or other natural sciences. Knight wrote,

> a natural science approach to social phenomena excludes any practical significance ... unless it assumes the point of view of a student and manipulator of the material studied who is outside of and apart from the material itself, and is active toward it while it is completely passive and inert toward him ... no (human) interest or problem is recognized in such a study except the 'idle curiosity' of the student, and of other students, if the results are communicated to others. (Knight 1935, 3)

Much later in his life, he continues this criticism of attempts to apply scientific techniques and mathematical analysis to economics, adding that ' ... the fundamental propositions and definitions of economics are neither observed nor inferred from observation in anything like the sense of the generalizations of the positive natural sciences or of mathematics ... ' (Knight 1940b, 154).

Knight does not, however, go so far as to relegate economics to the category of irrelevance. While he points out the differences between economics as a social science and the natural sciences, he is quick to state that economics nonetheless makes relevant observations about a conceptualized reality. He writes, ' ... they [the fundamental propositions and definitions of economics] are in no real sense arbitrary. They state "facts", truths about "reality" – analytical and hence partial truths about "mental" reality ... ' (Knight 1940b, 154).

This search for perfect, objective, and complete knowledge, or truth, is very much at the center of both Keynes' and Knight's thinking and at the very core of theology. Keynes' concern over the impact of uncertainty upon economic decision making suggests a clear understanding of the value and desirability of possessing perfect knowledge. Still, Keynes recognized that perfect knowledge is impossible, observing that because knowledge contains both subjective *and* objective elements,[10] complete knowledge remained unattainable.

Knight developed a significant relationship between uncertainty and the creation of economic profits and sought to understand this significance through a lifelong search for greater knowledge and 'truth'. The strong influence Knight had on his students was due to this search. One of his most successful disciples, George Stigler, wrote ' ... a major source of his influence was the strength of his devotion to the pursuit of knowledge. Frank Knight transmitted, to a degree I have seldom seen equaled, a sense of unreserved commitment to "truth"' (Stigler 1988, 17–18). Both Keynes and Knight were, however, concerned about the ethical ramifications of uncertainty, not just uncertainty itself, just as Adam Smith had recognized the ethical context of the coexistence of the dual role of individuals as motivated by self-interest and individuals as members of an organized society.

KNOWLEDGE AND RATIONAL BELIEF

Perhaps the most fundamental precept of classical economic theory is the notion that individual decision makers possess the inherent characteristic of rationality. From an economic standpoint, rationality assumes that consumers are in the possession of a well-ordered set of preferences and that they are able to achieve desired economic outcomes by making consumption decisions based upon this ordering, given their income or budget constraints. Rationality, therefore, suggests that consumers and investors are in possession of a reasonably high degree of knowledge about the future outcomes of current decisions.

To make sound, economically-efficient decisions, however, this knowledge must extend beyond the individual. It must include an awareness of economic variables in the present, as well as certain knowledge about the future state of those same economic variables. Furthermore, this knowledge must be complete, meaning that consideration must occur of every possible economic variable that may in any way affect the outcome in question.

Clearly, the ability of any economic agent to 'know' is impaired because such knowledge requires actuarial 'certainty'. It is virtually impossible for most economic decisions to be made in such a way that the resulting outcomes are economically efficient. For example, the existence of less than perfect certainty regarding the future and the outcome of future events, causes individuals to prefer the holding of some quantity of financial assets as a store of value against an uncertain future, rather than to direct more income toward consumption in the present. This preference for financial assets obviously has important negative ramifications upon the level of economic activity (Levine 1997, 6), ramifications that were recognized by Keynes.

Keynes and Knight, nonetheless, worked to develop economic theories that incorporated the existence of uncertainty. In order to develop theories, one must have an understanding of the external environment and its degree of predictability ('certainty') or unpredictability ('uncertainty'). This, in turn, is largely determined by the presence of some degree of order. It has been suggested that if one assumes the order of things to be operating in a predictable, even mechanical, and predefined manner, then the notion of a machine-like economic system can also be accepted (Dow 1994, 196).

Using Dow's analogy, a machine-like economic system can safely be assumed to be predictable. If the economy is a machine and if economic agents 'know' how it works, then the decisions made and actions taken by economic agents can reliably be used to develop an accurate prediction of future actions. If, indeed, an economy operates as a machine, certainty becomes a matter of fact. In statistical terms, an increasingly small coefficient of variation would result, since actual outcomes would become closer and closer to the expected outcome. If the mechanical view of the economic order is accepted, then certainty is accepted as a given, rather than as a result of belief (Dow 1994, 196).

Classical economic theory has evolved from the nineteenth-century notion of 'actual certainty' into a twentieth-century (and twenty-first) one in which certainty is not necessarily taken as a given, but is, nonetheless, the logical conclusion when probabilistic analysis is applied to situations in which various possible outcomes may result. While the future may not be known for certain, the future becomes probabilistically predictable. By applying probability analysis to questions of unknown future outcomes, uncertainty is reduced to a question of manageable risk (Knight 1921a, 20). This reflects the general understanding of classical economics as an economic model that is closed to external influences, and predictable by the use and acceptance of assumptions that include symmetric information and perfect knowledge. Such a system does not require or include any elements of theological content.

Perhaps in the less complex days in which the rudiments of classical theory were developed, this view could reasonably be accepted as true. The same cannot be said today as movement has occurred from this 'primitive' state of affairs, to a more sophisticated, advanced economy. Keynes identified the tools of classical economics as being those used to make Euclidean calculations in a non-Euclidean world (Keynes 1936, 16). The acceptance of this Euclidean, mechanical model perhaps made sense in a world characterized by a predominance of perfect competition. However, it does not accommodate the existence of uncertainty in the theoretical model of pure competition just as it does not accommodate uncertainty in the more realistic and more complex economic model of imperfect competition.

While Keynes did not embrace religion as an important or significant element within his own life, he did nonetheless respect its importance in guiding society and, as a result, in affecting economic behavior (Rymes 1994, 142). His concept of limited certainty, in fact, has elements of a theological basis in that, because of the limited extent of certainty within knowledge, knowledge itself becomes a matter of belief (Dow 1994, 203).

Without explicitly doing so, Keynes implies a theological dimension to his conceptualized reality when he claims that uncertainty cannot be completely eliminated by the application of statistical or probabilistic analysis. The theological influence is evident simply in the presence of uncertainty that is nonetheless acted upon. As Dow states, 'in order to act we must rely on convention and on intuition. To the extent that these have religious content, the implication is that the economic behavior has religious content' (Dow 1994, 199).

The influence upon Knight is much more obvious and, interestingly, much more negative. While Keynes was raised with little emphasis placed upon theology, other than how it might be replaced with man's more enlightened power of reason, Knight was brought up in a decidedly conservative and evangelical environment. Nonetheless, he ultimately rebels against these religiously conservative influences, claiming that theology, and especially organized religion, presents impediments in the way of a smoothly operating, market economy. Just as Keynes did, Knight incorporates a theological element into his conceptualized reality when he identifies uncertainty as the source of profit. Recognizing that decisions are made in an environment of conflict between the good of the individual and the good of society, Knight focuses much of his writing on such ethical issues.

THE INDIVIDUAL VERSUS SOCIETY

As was noted in Chapter 2, Keynes was significantly influenced by the philosophy of G.E. Moore. Of special interest to the present study of uncertainty and its ethical implication upon the economic theories of Keynes and Knight is the question of utilitarianism. G.E. Moore wrote

… this theory [utilitarianism] points out that all actions may, theoretically at least, be arranged in a scale, according to the proportion between the *total* quantities of pleasure or pain which they *cause*. And when it talks of the *total* quantities of pleasure or pain which an action causes, it is extremely important to realise that it means quite strictly what it says. We all of us know that many of our actions do cause pleasure and pain not only to ourselves, but also to other human beings ... the effects of our actions, in this respect, are often not confined to those which are comparatively direct and immediate, but that their indirect and remote effects are sometimes quite equally important or even more so.

Moore continues:

... in order to arrive at the *total* quantities of pleasure or pain caused by an action, we should, of course, have to take into account absolutely *all* of its effects, both near and remote, direct and indirect; and we should have to take into account absolutely *all* the beings, capable of feeling pleasure or pain, who were at any time affected by it .... (Moore 1903, 18–19)

Keynes took this quite literally to mean that individual decisions are not made in a vacuum. Decisions made by individual members of society affect other members of society. He observed that economists who accepted the precepts of the classical school had arrived at the erroneous conclusion that individual decision makers, seeking their own personal gain, would, nonetheless, make decisions that would ultimately serve the greater needs of society as well. He remarked

they [economists] have begun assuming a state of affairs where the ideal distribution of productive resources can be brought about through individuals acting independently by the method of trial and error in such a way that those individuals who move in the right direction will destroy by competition those who move in the wrong direction. (Keynes 1926, 282)

Keynes did not accept the idea that through some system of totaling the gains of some individuals and the losses of others would, in the end, result in a desirable social outcome. He recognized the uncivilized potential of actions taken based upon such a perspective.

The conventional wisdom, nonetheless, was one characterized by limited government involvement in economic affairs. Keynes noted ' ... this implies that there must be no mercy or protection for those who embark their capital or their labour in the wrong direction. It is a method of bringing the most successful profit-makers to the top by a ruthless struggle for survival, which selects the most efficient by the bankruptcy of the less efficient' (Keynes 1926, 282). Obviously Keynes viewed this attitude with distaste. His use of the phrases 'no mercy' and 'ruthless struggle for survival' can only be characterized as contemptuous of the Darwinian aspects of the *laissez-faire* philosophy.

While Keynes' policy recommendations will be discussed in Chapter 6, it should be noted here that Keynes was ultimately able to reconcile the needs of the individual and the needs of the society to which he belongs by proposing certain appropriate roles for government to play in directing the overall economy. Rather than leaving atomistic, individual decision makers open and vulnerable to the inhospitable forces of the free market, Keynes proposed a system of central actions designed to support the existing free-market system, while bringing it a higher degree of civility, and a higher degree of fairness.

ECONOMIC POWER VERSUS ECONOMIC FREEDOM

Knight wrote ' ... the good, according to utilitarians, is pleasure, which is a purely individual matter' (Knight 1929, 129). According to Knight, herein lies a fundamental point of conflict within a capitalist economic system characterized by *laissez-faire*. The basis of a free-market economy had, for hundreds of years, been based upon individually determined decisions, made by rational, utility-maximizing members of society. This was accepted as orthodoxy by virtually all mainstream economists. In the early years of the twentieth century, however, the question of whether this philosophy still held true emerged anew.

Knight's career, in fact, began at a time when economics was at a crossroads of its own. Knight's predecessors recognized the study of economics as encompassing historical, social, and moral issues. Inherent in this thinking was the acceptance of a God who created and directed the workings of the world in which economics took place. His contemporaries and many of his followers were those economists who preferred to think of economics as a positive science, capable of affecting the destiny of those using economics to direct their lives. Knight himself 'expresses the tension between the need to get on with the work of making sense of a world in which God is absent, while remaining acutely aware of what we have lost because God is no longer present' (Emmett 1994, 106).

Knight defined ethics in terms of moral values. He wrote that 'the values in question are moral values ... they are conduct values, or more specifically social relations in conduct, including relations in and between groups formally organized and acting as units' (Knight 1960, 153). Certain aspects of moral values, called *mores* by Knight, are static and unchanging. They are established, accepted, and historically-based ways of doing things within the society in question and are supported by institutions of that society, including such things as a system of law and order (Knight 1960, 25).

'Ethics' was the term used by Knight to refer to what he called 'progressive morality' or those moral values which change as a result of social progress (Knight 1960, 153). Ethics, then, are based upon dynamic concepts of change and a progressive movement forward. Knight had earlier written 'an organized system must operate in accordance with a social standard'. He viewed this standard as 'related in some way to the values of the individuals making up the society' (Knight 1923, 42). These values make their way into man's economic behavior by influencing the way in which individuals conduct themselves in pursuing means to the satisfaction of their wants and needs, including the way in which they prioritize and select from available alternatives (Knight 1923, 45).

Knight's analysis of the individual versus society is carried out through his consideration of economic freedom and economic power. Knight points out that political action had been relegated by the broad acceptance of utilitarianism to a role in which a government's limited actions enabled individuals to exert greater degrees of economic freedom. That is, the absence of governmental direction over economic affairs allowed individuals to possess greater freedom to direct their own affairs. From a utilitarian perspective, this suggests that the greatest good for society as a whole will be realized through the greatest possible degree of economic freedom (Knight 1929, 130).

Despite Knight's ultimate acceptance of *laissez-faire* and its inherent characteristic of utilitarian ethics, he nonetheless remained critical of the notion that the philosophy of utilitarianism was without flaw. 'The fatal defect in the utilitarian doctrine of maximum freedom as a goal of social policy', wrote Knight, 'is its confusion of freedom and power' (Knight 1929, 133). Knight believed that the supporters of a free-market utilitarian philosophy 'overlook the fact that freedom to perform an act is meaningless unless the subject is in possession of the requisite means of action, and that the practical question is one of power rather than of formal freedom' (Knight 1929, 133).

Since Knight's concern was the functioning of an economy within a democratic political system, he believed one of the strongest and most important characteristics was, nonetheless, freedom. In fact, Knight saw the existence of freedom as being the most important feature of *laissez-faire*. 'The supreme merit', wrote Knight, 'of the market-and-enterprise organization is that it embodies practically complete freedom – for the given individuals responsibly participating' (Knight 1960, 29). Knight thought of freedom as being equivalent in meaning to 'liberty', a word that he believed had been misused by economic policy makers of his day. He was critical of their use of the term 'liberalism', saying that 'it used to signify individual liberty, and now means rather state paternalism' (Knight 1960, 123). Knight therefore often used the term 'classical liberalism' to refer to the philosophy of *laissez-faire* rather than accepting its present-day meaning.

Knight believed that the individual freedoms that existed in a free-market economy were 'the major premise of liberal ethics' and that they provided for the 'right of every person to do as he will, without interference by any other' (Knight 1960, 123). But Knight was concerned that common thinking had concluded that with freedom must come 'power', or the ability to act upon one's desire to do as one freely chooses (Knight 1960, 16). This created an obvious ethical question for Knight, because he recognized that within a society made up of individuals or groups of individuals, for one person to act freely, meant that someone else's freedom could be imposed upon. He said 'even more am I puzzled about the rationality or moral quality of the activities of [a free-market economy] ... the end sought is to win, which cancels out, since for every victory there is a defeat' (Knight 1960, 109). The lives of the affected members of society were, in fact, not being lived entirely free and therefore freedom might somehow need to be limited to whatever degree was necessary to prevent the freedom of one individual from removing the freedom of another. He believed that people should be granted the freedom to direct their own actions 'as long as they do not interfere with the equal freedom of other people' (Knight 1960, 113).

Knight viewed a society claiming freedom to be progressive, because among its freedoms was the freedom to change. He viewed this progress to be evolutionary in nature, saying 'we have to look at human phenomena, at human history, in terms of emergent evolution' (Knight 1960, 42). This view was most likely influenced by the thinking of Max Weber, who is considered to be a major influence on Knight and who wrote that ' ... the capitalism of today ... educates and selects the economic subjects which it needs through a process of economic survival of the fittest' (Weber 1904, 55). Furthermore, Knight considered change to have occurred in the form of a 'continuous improvement of society' (Knight 1960, 149).[11] It was Knight's belief that these changes came about, in part, because of the values of society, revealing why Knight saw ethics as being so intimately related to questions of economics. Economic decisions such as quantities of production, income distribution, and resource allocation all hinge upon the value judgements of a free society, a society whose members must act intelligently and rationally in order to assure efficiency and a common level of welfare. This provided Knight with the basis for his lifelong struggle. He wrote 'behind and underlying concrete issues of economic policy lie deeper problems, of the nature of intelligent group action' (Knight 1960, 15).

The role of uncertainty and its accompanying ethical implications have been seen to appear in the economics of Knight and Keynes in a variety of ways. For both, the effect of uncertainty on the ability of economic agents to accurately predict the outcome of future events is obviously of significance. For Keynes, his well-known criticisms of *laissez-faire* and his belief that there was an appropriate role for collective action in economic matters was in response to his concern that individual 'money motive' decisions (including the holding of financial assets because of an uncertain future) could fail to achieve desired social economic objectives.

For Knight, his analysis of 'economic freedom versus economic power' followed much the same line as Keynes' concerns about the ability of an individual to act freely within a democratic market economy without infringing upon the rights and freedoms of others. Nonetheless, Knight believed that the ability of some individuals or businesses to accurately predict the outcome of an uncertain future brought about profit, which was their reward for doing so. Still, Knight remained convinced that overall, individuals lacked the ability to reduce uncertainty to probabilistic risk, a skill classical economic theory had assumed.

NOTES

1. William Leuchtenburg, in *The Perils of Prosperity 1914–32*, described the growing anti-capitalist sentiment that had emerged around the time of World War I. According to Leuchtenburg, many people went so far as to blame the selfish motives of capitalists for the global conflict. 'The only reasonable explanation [for the war] was that Europe had gone berserk. The European powers, declared the *New York Times*, "have reverted to the condition of savage tribes roaming the forests and falling upon each other in a fury of blood and carnage to achieve the ambitious designs of chieftains clad in skins and drunk with mead". If the war had any rational cause at all, Americans thought, it could be found in the imperialist lust for markets. "Do you want to know the cause of the war?" asked Henry Ford. "It is capitalism, greed, the dirty hunger for dollars. Take away the capitalist," Ford asserted, "and you will sweep war from the earth."' (Leuchtenburg 1958, 13).
2. See Davidson (1994), Skidelsky (1992).
3. Skidelsky says of Keynes' essay, 'Like all his best work, it is full of sparkling prose and arresting ideas.' Still, Skidelsky recognizes the essay's faults, ' … he lumps together, in briefest summary, objections to *laissez-faire* which may be philosophical or merely practical ('the prevalence of ignorance over knowledge'), moral objections (the 'cost … of the competitive struggle' and the 'tendency for wealth to be distributed where it is not appreciated most'), and objections which stem from changed techniques of production (economies of scale) leading to monopoly.' Nonetheless, Skidelsky recognized the importance of the essay when he observed ' … it remains the most impressive short attempt on record to define a social and economic philosophy fit for the time of troubles framed by the two world wars' (Skidelsky 1992, 225–8).
4. 'If I think of "*good*",' wrote Dewey, 'I am approaching conduct from the standpoint of value. I am thinking of what is desirable. This too is a standard, but it is a standard regarded as an end to be sought rather than as a law … it is an 'ideal'. The conscientious man, viewed from this standpoint, would seek to discover the true good, to value his ends, to form ideals, instead of following impulse or accepting any seeming good without careful consideration' (Dewey 1908, 7–8).
5. Locke argued that knowledge was not possessed automatically at birth, but comes about as a result of our life-experiences. Ultimately, these experiences congeal together into memories which, in turn, bring about ideas. In the end, Locke concludes that only material reality affects our senses. Therefore, man should adopt a philosophy based upon

material reality, understood through knowledge gained by the individual (Durant 1953, 256). Likewise, Hume argued that an individual's mind is nothing more than his own personal assembly of ideas, brought about not because of the presence of a 'soul' or by science, but because of our perceptions and that 'our certainties [are] but probabilities in perpetual danger of violation' (Durant 1953, 265).

6.   William Paley's *Principles of Moral and Political Philosophy* (1785) expressed the view that the hedonism of individuals extended to society as a whole. Paley believed that 'virtue' was typified by obeying the will of God, which was to do good for society as a whole. This philosophy reconciled for Paley the conflict between the individual and society (Paley 1785).

7.   See Stigler (1988) and Emmett (1992).

8.   In particular, Spencer was a pioneer in applying the theories of evolution (even before Darwin) to sciences other than biology. Spencer considered the social sciences to be the apex of scientific inquiry, and directed his work toward analyzing the framework of society and its individual members from the perspective of evolutionary inquiry, justifying economic freedoms by the argument of 'survival of the fittest' and 'natural selection' (Durant 1953, 361).

9.   Dow contends that economic theory develops in large part on 'an ontological judgment about the nature of the economic system'. Dow expresses the view that if one's economic theory is built around an economic system that is mechanical, or 'machine-like' (as with classical, orthodox economists), then it operates 'as if it were a closed system of deterministic relationships'. This view suggests that man has little need to exert control over the workings of the economy, since it is self-regulating and automatic in its operation. Alternatively, economic theory could be built around an economy that is part of a 'made' order, which 'evolves' and is not dependent upon internal, predetermined factors alone but is, in fact, susceptible to external forces and change (Dow 1994, 196–7).

10. Keynes believed that knowledge was partly objective because there were certain irrevocable, established facts that were independent of human interpretation and judgement. Knowledge was partly subjective because the scope and nature of human inquiry is of infinite duration and depth. This parallels his thinking about probability discussed in Chapter 3.

11. Knight is undoubtedly influenced by Thorstein Veblen's ideas on progress. Veblen wrote that ' ... change in the direction of what we call progress ... [is] in the direction of divergence from the archaic ... ' (Veblen 1899, 136).

5. The purpose and method of economics to Knight and to Keynes

Economics deals with the social organization of economic activity ... it is the structure and working of the system of free enterprise which constitutes the principal topic of discussion in a treatise on economics.
Frank H. Knight (1951)

Economics is a science of thinking in terms of models joined to the art of choosing models which are relevant to the contemporary world...good economists are scarce, because the gift for using 'vigilant observation' to choose good models, although it does not require a highly specialised intellectual technique, appears to be a very rare one.
John M. Keynes (1938)

At this point, it is necessary to move from detailed discussion of the concept of uncertainty within the economic theories of Knight and Keynes and turn to an examination of their respective views regarding the more general purpose and method of economics itself. Having explored the differing backgrounds of the two economists and the influences upon them, as well as their respective theories about uncertainty and its ethical implications, it is now appropriate to consider the *context* within which each economist developed his respective theories.

This context can be better understood in terms of Knight's and Keynes' opinions regarding the purpose and role of economic theory in general. As previously stated, the primary purpose of this book is to examine the question of why two economists who placed such an emphasis upon uncertainty could nonetheless arrive at such differing economic policy recommendations. It is therefore essential that the reader has an understanding not only of Knight's and Keynes' specific use of uncertainty, but also of their broader ideas about economics. This examination of the respective economic theories will nonetheless continue to be done with special focus and attention directed toward ethical and moral aspects that are relevant to the study at hand.

THE SOCIAL RELEVANCE OF ECONOMICS

Economics has been defined in a variety a different ways. In 1890 Alfred Marshall, perhaps the first modern economist to clearly set forth his understanding of how economics should be defined, stated 'Political Economy or Economics is a study of mankind in the ordinary business of life; it examines that part of individual and social action which is most closely connected with the attainment and with the use of the material requisites of wellbeing' (Marshall 1890, 1). More recently, Heilbroner and Milberg state: 'in its broadest sense, economics is the study of a process we find in all human societies – *the process of providing for the material well-being of society*' (Heilbroner and Milberg 1962, 1).

Within the context of the study at hand, an outstanding feature within these and many other definitions of economics is the emphasis put upon the place of the individual within his society. More so, it is especially important to note that there is a widely accepted recognition that economics does not exist merely to promote or to assist in achieving the utility-maximizing goals of self-interested individuals. Rather, economics exists as a *social science* whose primary purpose is to serve as a mechanism through which the limited resources of *society* are utilized in the most efficient way possible in providing for the economic well being of that *society*. Social well-being must not, however, be viewed as being limited to the fulfillment of material needs but must also include some consideration of freedom and justice. According to Frederic Bastiat, 'economics is the science of determining whether the interests of human beings are harmonious or antagonistic' (Bastiat 1850, 68).

The Benthamite calculus upon which classical economic theory came to be built was the product of an age in which the supremacy of the individual and his ability and even his right to direct his own actions was held as fundamental to human existence. Faith in the rationality of human beings led early classical economic thinkers such as Smith[1] and Ricardo to build theories that assumed individual actions would achieve the desired outcome of economic growth for society (macroeconomics). If only the government would leave the market to its own devices, this goal of economic growth would be the inevitable result. Later the marginalists,[2] Jevons, Menger, and Walras, shifted their emphasis to such economic issues as distribution of income, utility analysis and determination of value, and built their analysis upon individual (microeconomic) decisions. Marshall combined the work of these earlier economists, sythesizing the macroeconomics of the classicals with the microeconomics of the marginalists[3] (Brue 1963).

Nevertheless, throughout all this evolution of theory, the assumption of individual and collective rationality has remained intact. Interestingly, and despite the emphasis upon the supremacy of the individual, history is virtually devoid of any examples in which man can survive – and develop any sort of economic progress – in seclusion. Few individuals, if any, would be able to provide their own food, shelter, and clothing, if relying solely upon their own personal abilities to do so. It has been observed that it is 'our helplessness as economic individuals' that brings about the importance of recognizing the social relevance of economics (Heilbroner and Milberg 1962, 2).

SOCIAL ASPECTS OF KNIGHT'S ECONOMICS

First and foremost, Knight recognized that economics dealt with people. He observed that 'the problem of its scientific treatment involves fundamental problems of the relations between man and his world'. Knight did not merely believe that economics concerned itself with problems faced by man. He also believed that virtually *all* problems faced by man, at least all problems of any significance, were economic ones. 'From a rational or scientific point of view, all practically real problems are problems in economics. The problem of life is to utilize resources "economically," to make them go as far as possible in the production of desired results. The general theory of economics is therefore simply the rationale of life' (Knight 1935a, 105).

Knight identified economic principles as having two primary roles:

> ... these have, or surely ought to have, two kinds of significance: in explaining what does happen and in providing guidance for bringing about what is thought desirable or what ought to happen. In the first role they assimilate to principles of science; in the second, they raise questions of political principle, since action must be primarily political, and both economic and political principles are inseparable from ethics. (Knight 1951c, 256–7)

For Knight, economics served a historical role in bringing about a greater degree of understanding in terms of what has happened in the past and what is happening in the present within the realm of economic behavior and policy. This role exists alongside the part played by economic principles in guiding the formulation of future political and social action.

While Knight was clearly concerned with economic issues such as income distribution and the existence of imperfect competition, he was equally concerned with the ethical ramifications of economics in regard to the science's impact upon human behavior. In particular, Knight recognized the significance of economics in defining the respective roles of the individual within a society of free individuals. 'Economic principles are simply the more general implications of the single principle of freedom, individual and social, i.e., free association, in a certain sphere of activity' (Knight 1951c, 257).

The 'free association' to which Knight was referring was the existence of markets within which exchange occurred. Knight believed this exchange to be necessary because of the existence of the specialized division of labor. Because of the division of labor, it became necessary to engage in the exchange of one's own output for the output of another. Knight adds ' … the meaning of economics in the traditional or orthodox sense is the analysis of this system of co-operation in the production and distribution of impersonal goods' (Knight 1951c, 258). Cooperation, therefore, is viewed as an essential economic component of society.

Knight extends his analysis to define the task of economics to be 'to describe the structure and functioning of the economy, of the modern Western type, a free economy with markets and prices and private enterprise' (Knight 1960, 70). Knight was nonetheless highly critical of much of mainstream economic theory. He was especially critical of attempts by economists to apply scientific analysis, as was done in the natural sciences, to economic problems of society,[4] commenting that 'science … knowledge used for prediction and control – simply does not apply in a society with freedom and equality' (Knight 1960, 69). To Knight, the dynamic characteristics and unpredictability of economic issues differed from the static predictability of physics or chemistry.

This opinion is largely the result of Knight's view of human nature. He believed that 'people often behave romantically … which is in principle the opposite of behaving with economic rationality' (Knight 1960, 71). Since free individuals often did not act rationally or predictably, and because they suffer from ignorance, or worse, from ignorance of their own ignorance, Knight believed the questions of economics were social, dealing with relationships among individuals, and therefore they were ethically-based.[5] This ethical basis makes it difficult and even impossible to apply the mathematical methods of the natural sciences to the more unpredictable economic issues faced by 'romantic' individuals.

Compounding the problem, in Knight's opinion, is the presence of uncertainty within the economic reality faced by individuals and society. According to Knight, in the absence of uncertainty, society would be devoted solely 'to doing things'. Under this unrealistic assumption, intelligence need not exist. In the presence of uncertainty, which Knight believed to be characteristic of reality, ' … doing things, the actual execution of activity, becomes in a real sense a secondary part of life; the primary problem or function is deciding what to do and how to do it' (Knight 1921a, 268).

SOCIAL ASPECTS OF KEYNES' ECONOMICS

The similarities between Knight's and Keynes' opinions regarding the nature of economics are striking. Like Knight, Keynes did not believe economic analysis to fall within the realm of natural science techniques, because 'economics is essentially a moral science and not a natural science. That is to say, it employs introspection and judgments of value' (Keynes 1938a, 297). Nonetheless, Keynes never devoted an essay to the task of clearly outlining his conception of the nature of economics or of economic methodology, nor did he expend any significant effort in defining his conception of economics or its purpose. Rather, he spent most of his time exploring economic theory, spelling out his theories and suggestions for change. Keynes' work, nonetheless, is clearly written from the perspective of someone with well-defined ideas regarding the role and purpose of economics (O'Donnell 1989, 158). This role and purpose remains constant throughout his writings.

Keynes' private correspondence remains the best source for indications of his conceptions regarding the purpose and method of economics. It is from these letters that Keynes makes clear his position that economics is indeed a moral science. Like Knight, Keynes believed economics to lie outside the scope of the natural sciences, and that its primary purpose is as a tool for directing the efforts of individuals and of society in achieving long-term goals, especially as those goals relate to human well-being. Writing to Roy Harrod in 1938, Keynes contends 'it seems to me that economics is a branch of logic, a way of thinking; and that you do not repel sufficiently firmly attempts a la Schultz to turn it into a pseudo-natural-science' (Keynes 1938a, 296).

Keynes reached the conclusion that it was the inexact nature of economics that caused it to remain outside the bounds of the natural sciences. He identified the presence of irregularity, 'great difficulties of measurement and comparison … [high] interdependence with many other factors … [and] vagueness' as prevalent within the field of economics (O'Donnell 1989, 162). Likewise, he said ' … unlike the typical natural science, the material to which it [economics] is applied is, in too many respects, not homgeneous over time' (Keynes 1938a, 296). Due to these characteristics, the application of the mathematical techniques of the natural sciences serves only a limited function. Given this fact, said Keynes, it is unrealistic to even suggest that economics be considered anything but a social or moral science.

Of special interest to Keynes was the fact that economics deals with dynamic, changing aspects of society. Partially because of the dynamic nature of the real world, Keynes contended that the precepts of the classical economic models no longer provided adequate tools for practical analysis. To Harrod he continued ' … the grave fault of the later classical school … has been to overwork a too simple or out-of-date model' (Keynes 1938a, 296). Keynes was deeply concerned about the social ramifications of the rapid economic changes occurring in the early part of the twentieth century. He had previously written 'we are suffering just now from a bad attack of economic pessimism. It is common to hear people say that the epoch of enormous economic progress which characterized the nineteenth century is over; that the rapid improvement in the standard of life is now going to slow down … that a decline in prosperity is more likely than an improvement in the decade which lies ahead of us' (Keynes 1930b, 358). Keynes, therefore, denied the classical notion that full employment was the natural result of *laissez-faire*.

Keynes regarded the tendency of many contemporary economists to view economics as primarily concerned with individual decision making to be too narrow. His recognition of the social implications of economics is apparent when he identified his 'profound conviction that the Economic Problem, as one may call if for short, the problem of want and poverty and the economic struggle between classes and nations, is nothing but a frightful muddle, a transitory and an *unnecessary* muddle' (Keynes 1931, vii). Keynes did not view the role of economics as limited to the utility-maximizing decisions of individuals or to the profit-maximizing decisions of firms. He recognized the effect one group's decisions had on another, opting to consider the economy as a whole, rather than in parts.

The 'muddle' to which Keynes refers is the uneven distribution of income and wealth that is the result of the inability of the 'Western World' to allocate its resources efficiently and put its technology to use in a manner that results in the needs of its people being adequately met. He commented: ' … the Western World already has the resources and the technique, if we could create the organisation to use them, capable of reducing the Economic Problem, which now absorbs our moral and material energies … ' (Keynes 1931, vii). In order for the modern, contemporary world to face the Economic Problem effectively, Keynes suggested the application of economics.

It was Keynes' observation, however, that the Economic Problem could not be solved by the application of classical economic theories because 'economics is a science of thinking in terms of models joined to the art of choosing models which are relevant to the contemporary world … the object of a model is to segregate the semi-permanent or relatively constant factors from those which are transitory or fluctuating … ' (Keynes 1938a, 296). Keynes simply did not believe classical economics held the answers to the contemporary world's Economic Problem because the models of classical theory were no longer relevant. He proceeds to direct his efforts toward proposing what he believes to be the necessary improvements to economic theory so that the economic condition of society may be improved.

KNIGHT'S CONCEPTUALIZED REALITY

Despite Knight's criticism that methods commonly applied within the natural sciences should not (or could not) be applied to problems of economics, he nonetheless proposed that social problems could be analyzed, though not with the methods used in the natural sciences. He formulated, as other economists had done before him, a vision of the world, a conceptualized reality, to analyze the observed problems which he saw as plaguing free society. Knight viewed these economic problems as being fundamentally ethical in their foundation: 'economics and ethics naturally come into rather intimate relations with each other since both recognizedly deal with the problem of value' (Knight 1922, 19).

With this interrelation of ethics and economics in mind, Knight envisioned the world as consisting of two 'orders', the economic and the political (Knight 1960, 65). This separation of the sphere of economic matters from that of political issues, which had been especially evident since the latter part of the eighteenth century, resulted not in a great schism, but in a set of new social relationships. Herein lies Knight's most fundamental ethical concern. A society characterized by individual freedom, Knight feared, is full of problems brought on by human ignorance and prejudice. These imperfections must be considered by members of society in the determination of the degree to which its members should enjoy the benefits of freedom. Knight's concerns became focused upon the degree to which individuals should be free to make decisions for themselves, as in the case of a free-market economy, versus the degree to which collective action should be used to ensure that the decisions of individuals did not interfere with the rights of other members of society.

Because social relationships, by definition, involve the interaction of individuals, it is then necessary for Knight to identify the actors within his reality.[6] Knight suggested the existence of two kinds of men, the 'economic man' (Knight 1941c, 127) and the 'political man', who coexist within every individual (Knight 1960, 65). This individual in turn serves one of three roles within the economic order in addition to serving a role within the political order.[7]

Among the population of the economic order is the capitalist, who is the 'money lender' or the individual who provides money capital. There also exists the laborer, who sells his own labor services. It is not, Knight said, the capitalist who hires labor. Rather, a third economic actor, the entrepreneur, purchases the services of both. This, in effect, places capital and labor on the same organizational level, contrary to the theories of the earlier classical economists from whom Knight borrows so much underlying theoretical foundation (Knight 1951c, 258 and 1960, 66).

By placing the entrepreneur in such a central role, Knight revealed his conviction that this particular actor is of critical importance in his reality. This proved to be a significant factor in his ultimate acceptance of a free-market economic system. Nonetheless, Knight clearly acknowledges the importance of social interaction and of every individual within a free, democratic society. Having evolved to the point of possessing freedom, Knight again contends that each of these individuals must be competent enough to manage their own affairs and to make critical and intelligent decisions.

Knight's political order encompasses the process of politics, or as he called it 'the problem of leadership' (Knight 1934, 350). Within the political order, it is the political man's responsibility also to act with intelligence and reason, but Knight maintains his persistent concern that human nature precludes members of society from intelligent action as a group. He concludes that 'a large mass of people simply does not form a cohesive group and act as a unit ... on an intellectually critical basis; and intelligence must recognize this fact ... [political] leadership is an indefinitely more natural, an easier, and less costly system of order than any other' (Knight 1934, 352). Knight feared, however, that even the process of electing leaders had been reduced to a mindless process. He also became skeptical of the leadership abilities of members of the major political parties, finally threatening (perhaps idly) to vote for a Communist party candidate in order to bring about more significant change (Knight 1932).

Despite Knight's resentment of the tendency to apply the methods of the natural sciences to social issues, he contends that these new orders are nonetheless the subject of their own 'sciences'. Specifically, political science pertains to issues and conflicts within the political order while the science of economics deals with the economic order (Knight 1960, 66). The political and economic orders in turn form the basis of what can be called 'institutions' within Knight's reality.

The first institution, democracy, is a direct result of this movement away from governmental 'coercion' and influence over economic and social affairs. Knight accepted the definition of democracy as 'government by discussion' (Knight 1960, 2). Nonetheless, Knight also believed that the acceptance of this definition brought about many questions. Essentially, Knight believed there to be economic and social inefficiency resulting from the often incompetent government influence over economic affairs, but was concerned about the ethical dilemma of allowing a society with deeply ingrained prejudices to have complete freedom to direct its own affairs (Knight 1960, 7).

Free enterprise, the second institution within Knight's reality, is clearly evident in the economic order where markets and prices exist and where exchange occurs. It provides Knight with the core of his economic order, and the best illustration of his concern over the interrelationships of free individuals. While being at the heart of his economic order, free enterprise functions, by definition, within a democratic form of government. Again, here is a point of especially strong ethical content. He said: 'from the standpoint of social and political ethics, free enterprise in its theoretically ideal form is an embodiment and application of the fundamental principle of liberalism, i.e., individual liberty, including free association' (Knight 1946, 377).

Knight was concerned, nonetheless, that a large majority of the population did not really know what actions were in their best interest and, even if they did, they often acted contrarily to their own judgements. Furthermore, free enterprise, motivated by profit, could fall victim to the same problems as free individuals. That is, the freedom of one firm to compete in any way it chooses could prevent another from doing so. Lack of any government regulation or control was not, therefore, necessarily the best policy. This concern provided him with further reasons to examine critically the ethical soundness of a free-market economy.

The coexistence of individuals within these social institutions gave rise to certain values which Knight believed inherent in society and which conflicted with the policy of *laissez-faire* and its accompanying value of freedom. The first is *order*. To Knight, order precedes freedom and is the 'essence of any society' (Knight 1960, 154). Some form, and some degree of law and order is fundamentally necessary for any society to endure, but the existence of order inhibits the freedom of individuals. Second, is *security*, which Knight views as being analogous to and 'logically implied by order' (Knight 1960, 154). Likewise, security also conflicts with freedom since, 'freedom for one member of society means disorder and insecurity for others with whom he has dealings' (Knight 1960, 17).

Third, *efficiency* must be maintained as a value of a society in order for it to do more than simply survive. Knight accepted that for the quality of life to be improved, productive capability must be increased. This was true, even if the output of a society were merely to keep pace with a growing population (Knight 1960, 154). Likewise, *progress*, or the continued improvement of life for members of society must occur. According to Knight, freedom means freedom to change, which by definition includes progress. But 'progress also conflicts with order, and hence with literal freedom' (Knight 1960, 17). A society also requires economic efficiency in order to avoid wasteful utilization of resources. This necessitates the existence of a 'workable and effective economic organization' which provides for 'conservation and progress' (Knight 1960, 154).

Finally, a society requires the value of *justice*, which Knight called 'the most controversial of all' (Knight 1960, 154). A society must have a widely accepted measure of fairness in its economic and social affairs. Whether the questions at hand deal with income distribution or allocation of national product, or with fairness in dealing with criminal or civil offenses, justice must exist in order to prevent chaos.[8]

The existence of these values in Knight's reality reinforced his insistence that economic questions were really social questions, and as such, became ethical ones. Accordingly, Knight makes a plea for intelligent social action based upon an intelligent, non-prejudicial understanding of what is best for each individual and, in turn, society. He said:

> the most important field of social action ... and occasions by far the most controversy, is that of relations between the state as law and government and the market-and-enterprise organization of economic life. The problem is primarily moral, in the broad interpretation of progressive morals or ethics, and centers especially in economic or distributive justice. (Knight 1960, 156)

Knight differs from others in that his analysis of economic activity envisioned it as a complex system of human social interaction rather than as economic transactions occurring between individual agents or actors. Interestingly, it is this type of analysis that brought about Knight's ethical questions. As has been suggested in the preceding discussion, the basis for Knight's ethical analysis is freedom. He observed that as members of society moved from a state in which governmental authority had guided and directed significant aspects of their lives to one in which a greater degree of self-direction and self-governance prevailed, a new form of economic analysis became necessary in order to answer economic and social questions.

However, at the heart of the matter, Knight's fundamental ethical complaint against *laissez-faire* was that it did not provide society with any sort of common morality. It did not reveal a fundamental 'truth' from which appropriate individual and social actions could be determined. He believed it essential that members of society recognize this fact. 'The moral issues involved in the notion of truth affecting moral issues must be understood and faced,' Knight wrote, 'every honest worker for truth must recognize the moral limitations of human nature in himself as well as in others ... ' (Knight 1934, 354). Knight did not believe that members of a society, as a rule, possessed the intellect necessary to make socially beneficial decisions for themselves. Nor did he believe that the proponents of such a system recognized the fact that certain essential 'knowledge' was lacking from the members of society who were thrust into a capitalistic, competitive system.

Knight said, 'the distinctive virtue for men in free society, the essence of the whole liberal view of life, is truth-seeking' (Knight 1960, 14). He believed that intelligent action in a democratic, free-market society required knowledge of what is right, or best, not for the individual, but for society. Knight is careful to point out that this does not mean 'moralizing' or holding that any 'truth' is not open to question. Rather, he recommends the pursuit of knowledge through education and that this is an appropriate role for government within a free democracy. He says 'with respect to political action in the economic sphere, the main task of society, at the present juncture, is education, but of the will more than the intellect; it is to develop a more critical attitude' (Knight 1960, 14). Furthermore, Knight saw education's major priority to be 'to "unteach", to overcome prejudice and the inclination to snap judgments and develop the will to be intelligent, i.e., intelligent and critical' (Knight 1960, 4). He goes on to say that, 'the first step is to make people in general more critical, less romantic, in their judgments of debating arguments used in political campaigns, and of advertising and sales-talk' (Knight 1960, 13).

In the hope of minimizing the effect of these ethical problems, Knight prescribed three 'commandments' to be followed if intelligent action were to be the desired result.

First, 'compare the alternatives' (Knight 1960, 154). Knight believed it essential that alternatives be identified and evaluated. This would slow the decision-making process, avoiding what he called 'snap judgments'. Second, 'appraise the alternative', through objective evaluation, and third, 'act on the basis of the best knowledge or judgment that is had' (Knight 1960, 154).

Knight clearly believed that decisions should not be made, or action taken, unless it can be done intelligently. Moreover, he believed that certain knowledge was required for intelligent action to be taken. Decision makers who are acting intelligently must first be aware of or able to predict the outcome if no action were taken at all. Decision makers must also be aware of their capabilities and limitations, given current circumstances and available resources, and must also be aware of all possible 'consequences' of their action. Finally, decision makers must be able to compare the possible outcomes and evaluate the relative costs and benefits of each (Knight 1960, 146). Given these criteria for intelligent action, Knight was often less than optimistic that such action could be achieved, at least by individual members of society. It was Knight's position that 'knowledge and the possibility of knowledge adequate for rational behavior are limited' (Knight 1960, 146). Still, Knight recognized that 'predictive' knowledge is required for rational decisions to be made. He held this to be especially problematic for the 'individual' but less so for 'society' as a whole. It was Knight's opinion that the problem of adequate predictive knowledge is ' ... relevant chiefly for intelligent individual activity aimed at redirecting the course of natural events. It has little application to social action, because of radical differences in the nature of the problem' (Knight 1960, 148).

As a result, while Knight remained generally supportive of *laissez-faire*, he ultimately came to accept the proposition that collective (social) action could be used to correct for imperfections in the economic system. These imperfections prohibit a free-market economy from achieving the greatest good for the greatest number. To Knight,

> social action means political action, which in a democracy means action by government, in accord with laws, made as well as enforced by a government consisting of persons held responsible to the people, the electorate of normal adults. The alternative is literally free action by the individual members of society or – actually, for the most part – by groups formed through voluntary association to promote common interests. (Knight 1960, 161)

These common interests center upon society's primarily goal, which, according to Knight is ' ... simply the continuous improvement of society ...' (Knight 1960, 149). Knight's policy recommendations are directed toward achieving this improvement, through a determination of the appropriate degree of social or collective action required to facilitate the functioning of a free-market economy while ensuring the attainment of continued progress for society. The details of Knight's policy recommendations follow in Chapter 6.

KEYNES' CONCEPTUALIZED REALITY

The economic model envisioned by Keynes had as its primary objective the goal of explaining the existence of prolonged periods of involuntary unemployment. Denying the validity of Say's Law,[9] Keynes succinctly identified the most fundamental aspect of his model when he wrote

> put very briefly, the point is something like this. Any individual, if he finds himself with a certain income, will, according to his habits, his tastes and his motives towards prudence, spend a portion of it on consumption and the rest he will save. If his income increases, he will almost certainly consume more than before but it is highly probable that he will also save more. That is to say, he will not increase his consumption by the full amount of the increase in his income. Thus if a given national income is less equally divided, or, if the national income increases so that individual incomes are greater than before, the gap between total incomes and the total expenditure on consumption is likely to widen. (Keynes 1934, 489)

Say's Law, therefore, cannot hold in a monetary economy in which the marginal propensity to consume is less than one. Keynes saw the cause of this propensity to save as being rooted in the recognition and acceptance of an uncertain and unpredictable future.[10]

The inevitable outcome of this gap, observed Keynes, is an increasing level of unemployment, leading to what Keynes called the 'outstanding fault of the economic society', specifically, 'its failure to provide for full employment and its arbitrary and inequitable distribution of wealth and incomes' (Keynes 1936, 372). This inequitable distribution takes place among the economic actors of Keynes' conceptualized reality, a reality highly influenced by Alfred Marshall's theories of human nature, social, and industrial organization (Jensen 1983, 70–71).

The primary actors within Keynes' conceptualized reality are rentiers, entrepreneurs, laborers, and consumers. In Keynes' reality, rentiers own the capital assets of businesses. These capitalists are what Keynes calls the 'professional investor and speculator'. In Keynes' eyes, the rentiers present an especially important moral and ethical dilemma. They are concerned 'not with making superior long-term forecasts of the probable yield of an investment over its whole life, but with foreseeing changes in the conventional basis of valuation a short time ahead of the general public' (Keynes 1936, 154). Keynes continues, 'they are concerned, not with what an investment is really worth to a man who buys it "for keeps", but with what the market will value it at, under the influence of mass psychology, three months or a year hence' (Keynes 1936, 155).

This short-term investment valuation is highly influenced by the tendency of investment markets to express a favorable tendency toward liquidity. This preference for liquidity, according to Keynes, results in business decisions being made almost solely to ' … "beat the gun", as the Americans so well express it, to outwit the crowd, and to pass the bad, or depreciating, half-crown to the other fellow' (Keynes 1936, 155). Keynes believed the pursuit of short-term profit came at the expense of a preferred and perhaps higher long-term valuation and that 'the social object of skilled investment should be to defeat the dark forces of time and ignorance which envelop our future' (Keynes 1936, 155). Again, Keynes views ignorance of the future (uncertainty) as a significant factor in causing individuals to prefer the perceived safety of liquidity which, in turn, affects the level of investment and, in turn, the level of economic activity. The ethical and moral consequences of this propensity are indeed significant.

A second actor within Keynes' reality is the entrepreneur, who manages, but does not own, the business enterprise. The entrepreneur directs his efforts toward those activities that will maximize the potential future yield from real capital assets, which he has placed into productive service. It is the entrepreneur who seeks financial capital from the rentier. The entrepreneur receives an income[11] as compensation for bringing together the factors of production and assuming the risk involved in doing so. Keynes places great importance upon the income of the entrepreneur. It is the entrepreneur who, in large measure, determines the income not only of himself but also of the entire community. Given Keynes' definition of the entrepreneur's income as being equal to:

$$A - F - U = \text{Entrepreneur's income} \qquad (5.1)$$

Where: A = Total Revenue
                          F = Factor Cost
                          U = User Cost

then:

$$A - U = \text{Entrepreneur's income} + F = \text{Aggregate income} \qquad (5.2)$$

Aggregate income is equal to both entrepreneurial income plus the entrepreneur's factor cost (F), which represents the income of everyone else. It is the efforts of the entrepreneur to maximize his income that, in turn, results in his hiring of other factors of production, bringing income and employment to the providers of labor and of other productive resources (Keynes 1936, 54). This places the entrepreneur at perhaps the most critical juncture, from a technical as well as an ethical perspective, in the process of wage determination.

The third actor within Keynes' reality is the propertyless worker. The worker sells his labor services to entrepreneurs in exchange for a wage. Keynes observed that, according to classical theory, there are two basic postulates upon which the determination of wages and the level of employment are based. The first postulate is that 'the wage is equal to the marginal product of labour' and the second that, 'the utility of the wage when a given volume of labour is employed is equal to the marginal disutility of that amount of employment' (Keynes 1936, 5).

In the case of the former, classical employment theory stated that the value of the additional output produced by one additional worker is equal to the wage. In the case of the latter, the real wage is just sufficient to entice the worker to sell his labor rather than withhold it from the labor market. The level of employment, according to classical theory, was therefore determined by an 'equilibrium' between the two postulates. Keynes observed that 'the first [postulate] gives us the demand schedule for employment, the second gives us the supply schedule; and the amount of employment is fixed at the point where the utility of the marginal product balances the disutility of the marginal employment' (Keynes 1936, 6). Keynes recognized that this was compatible with the existence of 'frictional' and 'voluntary' unemployment,[12] but he came to reject classical theories of employment in the face of prolonged, high levels of what he called 'involuntary' unemployment, which he did not believe the postulates could explain (Keynes 1936, 6). Rather, Keynes identifies the point of effective demand[13] in the product markets as the factor determining the demand for labor (Davidson 1998, 817).

Involuntary unemployment of labor became an issue with which Keynes was very much concerned. The postulates of classical theory supported the notion that the high levels of unemployment, typical of periods of recession and depression, were the result of labor's refusal to accept a lower nominal (money) wage. It was Keynes' observation that the facts of the real world simply did not support this claim. Specifically, Keynes wrote ' ... the contention that the unemployment which characterises a depression is due to a refusal by labour to accept a reduction of money-wages is not clearly supported by the facts' (Keynes 1936, 9). The existence of significant fluctuations in the volume of employment without any significant change in the marginal disutility or the marginal product of labor was sufficient evidence for Keynes to contend 'these facts from experience are a *prima facie* ground for questioning the adequacy of the classical analysis' (Keynes 1936, 9).

Keynes' objections to the wage and employment theories of classical economic theory[14] were therefore based upon his belief that a decrease in real wages because of inflation did not cause the supply of labor to fall from the level employed before the period of inflation. According to Keynes, ' ... to suppose that it does is to suppose that all those who are now unemployed though willing to work at the current wage will withdraw the offer of their labour in the event of even a small rise in the cost of living' (Keynes 1936, 13). Additionally, and more fundamentally, Keynes disagreed with the assumption that the level of real wages is determined by the wage bargain between entrepreneurs and laborers, rather than the level of output, employment and the real wage being co-determined by the point of effective demand, as Keynes himself proposed (Davidson 1998, 825).

Recognizing the existence of 'social friction' between the rentier and labor, Keynes suggested that during periods of economic progress it is better for money wages to increase as a result of increased efficiency rather that to remain stable and allow prices to fall (Keynes 1930a, 127). Keynes viewed the 'psychological' difference between rising money wages and falling prices to be important enough to comment that ' ... I think that earners are more satisfied if, when they become more efficient, they benefit in the shape of higher wages than if they benefit by lower prices' (Keynes 1930a, 129).

It is Keynes' objection to the application of classical theory to the problems of the 'real' world that contrast so drastically with those of orthodox economists, including Knight. Keynes remarked ' ... if the classical theory is only applicable to the case of full employment, it is fallacious to apply it to the problems of involuntary unemployment – if there be such a thing (and who will deny it?)' (Keynes 1936, 16).

Uniting Keynes' three major economic actors is the consumer household. Each consumer household is composed of some combination of rentiers, entrepreneurs, and workers, as well as their families. In Keynes' conceptualized reality, each individual therefore serves a dual purpose of being either the provider of capital, management skill, risk taking, or labor in addition to assuming the role of a consumer of finished products and services.

It is within the institution of the household that the catalyst for Keynes' ethical concerns becomes a significant and relevant issue. As was previously mentioned, Keynes was concerned about the propensity of consumers to save a portion of their income when he referred to their 'habits', 'tastes', and 'motives toward prudence' (Keynes 1934, 489). These factors combine to produce a tendency for consumers to spend something less than their entire income. Keynes called this tendency the 'psychological propensity to consume' and it is this propensity that provides Keynes with yet another point of disagreement with classical theory, namely Say's Law. Keynes recognized that the liquidity preferences of individuals led them to make choices in which they refrained from spending their entire income, ultimately causing effective demand to fall short of the level required to maintain full employment.

Keynes contended that the propensity to consume is relatively stable and that the level of aggregate consumption is largely dependent upon the level of aggregate income (Keynes 1936, 96). Keynes believed that ' ... men are disposed, as a rule and on the average, to increase their consumption as their income increases, but not by as much as the increase in their income' (Keynes 1936, 96). So constant is the tendency for individuals to exhibit a marginal propensity to consume of less than one, that Keynes dubbed this behavior a 'fundamental psychological law'. He considered this propensity to be the result of the way in which consumers responded to uncertainty and in turn the mechanism through which they satisfy their preference for liquidity. Specifically, it was Keynes' observation that consumers prefer to hold some portion of their earned income in the form of liquid assets. This conclusion is based upon what Keynes called ' ... our knowledge of human nature and from the detailed facts of experience' (Keynes 1936, 96).

He held this observation to be especially true in the short run, where 'cyclical fluctuations of employment' result in a situation in which 'habits, as distinct from more permanent psychological propensities, are not given time enough to adapt themselves to changed objective circumstances' (Keynes 1936, 97). It was Keynes' belief that an individual's income goes first to maintaining the standard of living to which the individual has become accustomed. The difference between an individual's actual income and this predetermined 'habitual' standard is saved. Keynes therefore believed that increased saving would accompany a higher income and that savings would be decreased when faced with a lower income, at least in the short-run (Keynes 1936, 97).

Yet another point made by Keynes in relation to the propensity to consume has important ethical ramifications. Keynes not only recognized the existence of the propensity to consume, but he also extended his analysis to suggest that the propensity to consume is, in fact, a diminishing propensity to consume. Specifically, Keynes believed that the marginal (and average) propensity to consume would be greater at lower levels of income than at higher level ones.[15] Keynes wrote ' ... a rising income will often be accompanied by increased saving, and a falling income by decreased saving, on a greater scale at first than subsequently' (Keynes 1936, 97). This application of marginal analysis has an important ramification related to questions of an equitable income distribution, regarded by Keynes as one of the evils of capitalism.

Keynes was puzzled by the 'paradox of poverty in the midst of plenty' and used his analysis of the marginal propensity to consume as an explanation of this phenomenon. Keynes' concluded that it is 'the propensity to consume and the rate of new investment [that] determine between them the volume of employment ... ' (Keynes 1936, 30). Since individuals often prefer the holding of cash balances in lieu of current consumption, it is necessary for new investment to compensate for the shortfall in effective demand. According to Keynes, 'if the propensity to consume and the rate of new investment result in a deficient effective demand, the actual level of employment will fall short of the supply of labour potentially available at the existing real wage, and the equilibrium real wage will be *greater* than the marginal disutility of the equilibrium level of employment' (Keynes 1936, 30). This 'insufficiency of effective demand' could potentially slow or bring to a complete stop any growth in employment before the point of full employment is reached.

Specifically, it was Keynes' contention that the aggregate level of income and employment could be raised if only changes could be made to the distribution of income such that the overall propensity to consume were increased. Keynes believed that 'our habit of withholding from consumption an increasing sum as our incomes increase' meant that the aggregate income of society could not increase since the result of this behavior is insufficient effective demand to maintain current production levels (Keynes 1934, 490). Especially troubling to Keynes is his belief that, because of its inherently lower marginal propensity to consume, ' ... the richer the community, the wider will tend to be the gap between its actual and its potential production; and therefore the more obvious and outrageous the defects of the economic system' (Keynes 1936, 31).

Contrary to theories of a self-correcting economic system, Keynes did not believe it was possible for automatic adjustments[16] to restore the economy to a level of full-employment. Rather, Keynes suggested 'there is no theoretical reason for believing it [classical theory] to be true. A very moderate amount of observation of the facts, unclouded by preconceptions, is sufficient to show that they do not bear it out' (Keynes 1934, 490). Keynes suggested that ' ... the only remedy is for us to change the distribution of wealth and modify our habits in such a way as to increase our propensity to spend our incomes on current consumption' (Keynes 1934, 490) because ' ... there is a strong presumption that a greater equality of incomes would lead to increased employment and greater aggregate income' (Keynes 1934, 491). According to Keynes ' ... none of this, however, will happen by itself or of its own accord. The system is not self-adjusting, and, without purposive direction, it is incapable of translating our actual poverty into our potential plenty' (Keynes 1934, 491).

Keynes recognized, however, the controversial nature of his recommendations. Despite arguing for ' ... the maintenance of prosperity and civil peace on policies of increasing consumption by a more equal distribution of incomes ... ', Keynes admitted that 'there will be many social and political forces to oppose the necessary change ... ' (Keynes 1937b, 132). Keynes accepted the reality that much of society would be reluctant to adopt economic policy changes based upon theories other that those of the established, classically based orthodoxy. Keynes wrote, 'it is probable that we cannot make the changes wisely unless we make them gradually' (Keynes 1937b, 132).

According to Keynes, these gradual changes must ultimately lead to a more equal distribution of income and a rate of interest low enough to encourage higher levels of investment. Keynes feared a situation in which ' ... capitalist society rejects a more equal distribution of incomes and the forces of banking and finance succeed in maintaining the rate of interest ... ' such that ' ... a chronic tendency towards the underemployment of resources must in the end sap and destroy that form of society' (Keynes 1937b, 132). Keynes' economic policy recommendations incorporate his conviction that the distribution of income must become more equitable and that the central banking authority must take appropriate action to assure adequate private investment. These policy recommendations will be explored more fully in Chapter 6.

ECONOMICS AS THE MEANS OF IMPROVING THE HUMAN CONDITION

Both Knight and Keynes recognized glaring ethical problems inherent within a free-market economy. Likewise, both Knight and Keynes recognized that the social science of economics could be used as a means to improve the human condition. Each contended in his own way that the use of economic analysis led to a greater understanding of the individual and collective actions that should be taken in order for mankind to achieve an improved, socially desirable state of being.

Knight's Plea for Intelligence in Social Action

Knight's use of economic analysis is largely from the perspective of ' ... the political policy of *laissez faire*, i.e., simply *free* co-operation or mutual consent in all joint activity in the use of any means to achieve any end' (Knight 1948, 291). It was Knight's contention that this understanding and use of economics required an acceptance of 'the ethical principle of freedom'. In turn, the acceptance of freedom as an ethical precept required the acceptance of the notion that people are free, or should be free, to make their own choices as long as those choices did not interfere with the rights of others to make *their* own choices as well. This implies the acceptance of a role for government in which its primary function is to prevent those choices of individuals that interfere with the rights of others.

Knight therefore suggests that economics ' ... is relative to this policy and this ethic. Its function is to show by analysis of market competition how freedom of exchange works out automatically (without central control) to an organization of production and distribution ... ' (Knight 1948, 291). Likewise, Knight's recognition that economics has 'two kinds of significance: in explaining what does happen and in providing guidance for bringing about what is thought desirable or what ought to happen ... ' (Knight 1951c, 256) reveals that he maintained the belief that economics should be utilized in such a way that the economic condition of man could be improved through its appropriate application.

Despite Knight's general support for a system of *laissez faire*, he remained critical of what he viewed as the most significant problem resulting from a free-market economic system. Specifically, he pointed out that the problem of 'unequal distribution of productive capacity' was the 'economic problem that lies nearest the surface' (Knight 1948, 295). This 'productive capacity' arises out of the existence of financial, physical, and human capital. Knight observed that those individuals in possession of such capital are in a position to produce still more capital. The major difficulty arising from this circumstance is that 'there is a tendency for inequality to increase cumulatively' (Knight 1948, 295).

For Knight, economics serves as a mechanism through which more intelligent individual, political and social actions can be taken. Economic problems, thought Knight, are primarily ones that 'arise out of conflicts due to limitation of resources in relation to total needs or wants, and these are social problems when the ends are those of different people' (Knight 1946, 326). The ultimate purpose of economics is therefore to enable society to utilize in the best way possible, all of the material things in its possession 'through comparison, selection, and combination of competing alternative ends ... ' (Knight 1946, 326). Economic principles, while not perfectly applicable to matters of human nature as scientific principles are to the natural sciences, nevertheless remain useful in this endeavor.

According to Knight, this process of comparison and selection between alternatives must occur through the mechanism of social action, which 'is a matter of achieving desirable social changes and avoiding changes which are undesirable' (Knight 1946, 327). To achieve this somewhat utilitarian end, Knight suggested the application of economics in order to bring about the necessary improvements and corrections to problems facing society because of imperfections in its existing free-market economic system.

Keynes' Transmutation of the Money-Making Passion

Keynes believed his restatement of economic theory would reveal certain flaws in the classical economic theory that until his time had come to be widely accepted. He introduced his *General Theory* with the observation that ' ... if orthodox economics is at fault, the error is to be found not in the superstructure, which has been erected with great care for logical consistency, but in a lack of clearness and of generality in the premises' (Keynes 1936, v). Keynes' objective within *The General Theory* was to convince economists to reexamine critically not merely the classical economic theories so many of them had come to accept. As has been previously indicated, he wanted their attention to be directed toward certain fundamental assumptions underlying classical theory that he considered to be unrealistic.

Furthermore, it was Keynes' hope that 'the practical influence of economic theory' could be restored by his efforts to close the rift that existed within the economics profession between his 'fellow economists', which caused the general public to dismiss economics as merely an academic exercise (Keynes 1936, vi). It was Keynes' hope that economic theory, from his 'new' perspective, might bring about a distribution of income more equitable than was the present case and that relations between nations could be improved in the absence of economic disagreement. Keynes was quick to point out that he believed there to be ' ... social and psychological justification for significant inequalities of incomes and wealth, but not for such large disparities as exist to-day' (Keynes 1936, 374.)

Keynes hoped to show that it is not the 'abstinence of the rich' that brings about the growth of wealth, but that such abstinence from consumption actually *slows* the growth of wealth (Keynes 1936, 371). By making this observation, Keynes effectively removes a fundamental argument *for* an uneven distribution of income. Nonetheless, Keynes recognized the importance of maintaining some moderate degree of income inequality in order to maintain some measure of personal incentive. For Keynes, the degree of income inequality to be allowed was a question of social and individual ethics.

Keynes recognized that 'dangerous human proclivities' will be directed toward the pursuit of profit and financial gain in one way or another. If this 'proclivity' can be channeled within a free-market, capitalistic system, with adequate social controls, this would be preferable to allowing them to ' ... find their outlet in cruelty, the reckless pursuit of personal power and authority, and other forms of self-aggrandisement. It is better that a man tyrannise over his bank account than over his fellow-citizens' (Keynes 1936, 374.)

It was Keynes' desire to redirect the role of economics toward providing society with an important tool in reaching a level of economic well-being that would release individuals from undue concern over their finances. While this did not mean the death of capitalism, it did mean that certain parameters should be in place to assure fairness and equity. Keynes wrote, ' ... the task of transmuting human nature must not be confused with the task of managing it ... it may still be wise and prudent statesmanship to allow the game to be played, subject to rules and limitations, so long as the average man, or even a significant section of the community, is in fact strongly addicted to the money-making passion' (Keynes 1936, 374).

The foregoing discussion of the conceptualized economic realities of Knight and Keynes must be framed within an understanding of their more general view of the real world itself. Specifically, the economic actors and institutions within their respective models carry out their activities in the face of an uncertain future. For Keynes, uncertainty is evident in a world of true non-ergodicity, in which the future is simply unknowable. For Knight, an otherwise ergodic world is unknowable because of some inherent limitation within the economic actors themselves. This distinction becomes critically important as Knight and Keynes develop policy recommendations in the hope of improving the future of society, seeking to find a cure for the prevailing economic problems.

NOTES

1. Smith concluded: ' ... every system which endeavours, either, by extraordinary encouragements, to draw towards a particular species of industry a greater share of the capital of the society than what would naturally go to it; or, by extraordinary restraints, to force from a particular species of industry some share of the capital which would otherwise be employed in it; is in reality subversive of the great purpose which it means to promote. It retards, instead of accelerating, the progress of the society towards real wealth and greatness ... all systems either of preference or of restraint, therefore, being thus completely taken away, the obvious and simple system of natural liberty establishes itself of its own accord' (Smith 1776, 391).
2. While Jevons, Menger, and Walras followed similar lines of inquiry, Jevons and Menger concentrated on a line of causation from utility to value of both final goods and factors of production. Walras recognized the interdependence of value determination between final goods and factors of production, focusing his analysis on a 'general equilibrium' rather than on utility itself (Landreth and Colander 1994, 277).
3. Specifically, Marshall believed both supply (cost of production) *and* demand (marginal utility) contributed to the determination of value, depending upon the time frame under consideration. He wrote, ' ... we may conclude that, *as a general rule*, the shorter the period which we are considering, the greater must be the share of our attention which is given to the influence of demand on value; and the longer the period, the more important will be the influence of cost of production on value' (Marshall 1890, 349). Interestingly, Marshall appeared to provide Keynes with points of both agreement as well as disagreement. On the point of uncertainty, Marshall wrote, ' ... we cannot foresee the future perfectly ... the unexpected may happen ... the fact that the general conditions of life are not stationary is the source of many of the difficulties that are met with in applying economic doctrines to practical problems' (Marshall 1890, 347). But Marshall also wrote, ' ... when demand and supply are in stable equilibrium, if any accident should move the scale of production from its equilibrium position, there will be instantly brought into play forces tending to push it back to that position ... ' (Marshall 1890, 346). In the case of the former, Keynes agreed to such an extent that much of his work is built upon acceptance of uncertainty and the recognition that it has a significant impact upon economic behavior. In the case of the latter can be found one of Keynes' fundamental disagreements with classical economic theory.
4. For example, Knight was intensely opposed to the Vienna Circle's claim of the late 1920s that social sciences, including economics, should incorporate the same methodology as the natural sciences (Hands 1997, 196).
5. According to Schweitzer, it was Knight's predilection for discussing ethical principles that justifies the categorization of so much of his work within the realm of social economics (Schweitzer 1975, 283).
6. In addition to those references cited regarding Knight's economic actors and institutions, see Knight 1951a, especially pp. 31– 66 for additional discussion.

7. This is indicative of Knight's self-admitted pluralistic approach to economics, with Knight recognizing the simultaneous coexistence of physical, biological, and social within each individual member of society (Hands 1997, 199).

8. According to Bastiat, 'immediately following the development of a science of economics, and at the very beginning of the formulation of a science of politics, this all-important question must be answered: What is law? What ought it to be? What is its scope; its limits? Logically, at what point do the just powers of the legislator stop? I do not hesitate to answer: *Law is the common force organized to act as an obstacle to injustice.* In short, *law is justice*' (Bastiat 1850, 68).

9. Specifically, Keynes denied the validity of Say's Law within a monetary economy, regardless of the monetary authority's prevailing policy as well as in the case of an inelastic money supply. Keynes' denial of Say's Law was largely based upon his liquidity preference theory that individuals would hold money balances in the face of an uncertain future (Hansen 1953, 130).

10. This remains the major reason for Keynes' attempt to break from the 'habitual mode of thought' prevalent within orthodox economics. Keynes wrote 'I sum up, therefore, the main grounds of my departure as follows: (1) The orthodox theory assumes that we have a knowledge of the future of a kind quite different from that which we actually possess. This false realization follows the lines of the Benthamite calculus. The hypothesis of a calculable future lead to a wrong interpretation of the principles of behavior which the need for action compels us to adopt, and to an underestimation of the concealed factors of utter doubt, precariousness, hope and fear' (Keynes 1937a, 20). Actually, Keynes was skeptical that anyone remained who still accepted Say's Law: 'I doubt many modern economists really accept Say's Law that supply creates its own demand ... they have not been aware that they were tacitly assuming it ... the psychological law underlying the Multiplier has escaped unnoticed' (Keynes 1937a, 21).

11. Keynes defines the income received by the entrepreneur as 'the excess of the value of his finished output sold during the period over his prime cost' (Keynes 1936, 53). The 'prime cost' is the total of the amounts paid to the providers of any factor of production (factor cost) in addition to the value of purchases made to vendors for finished goods plus the net cost of capital equipment (user cost).

12. Keynes viewed frictional unemployment to be the result of 'various inexactnesses of adjustment which stand in the way of continuous full employment' and voluntary unemployment to be 'due to the refusal or inability of a unit of labour, as a result of legislation or social practices or of combination for collective bargaining or of slow response to change or of mere human obstinacy, to accept a reward corresponding to the value of the product attributable to its marginal productivity' (Keynes 1936, 6).

13. Keynes defines effective demand as ' ... simply the aggregate income (or proceeds) which the entrepreneurs expect to receive, inclusive of the incomes which they will hand on to the other factors of production, from the amount of current employment which they decide to give' (Keynes 1936, 55). Also Keynes asserted, 'the value of D [expected proceeds from a given level of employment] at the point of the aggregate demand function, where it is intersected by the aggregate supply function, will be called *the effective demand*' (Keynes 1936, 25).

14. Specifically those of Professor Pigou, whose *Theory of Unemployment* Keynes identified as 'the only detailed account of the classical theory of employment which exists' (Keynes 1936, 7).

15. According to Alvin Hansen, this is a point in which Keynes erred. Hansen points out that Keynes 'confuses the *level* of the consumption with the *slope* of the consumption function'. Hansen emphasizes the point that while the *average* propensity to consume may be higher in a poor country and lower in a wealthy country, it does not necessarily follow that their *marginal* propensity to consume would likewise be higher in a poor country and lower in a wealthy country. According to Hansen, 'Keynes was not sufficiently careful here (as elsewhere) to distinguish between the average and the marginal propensity to consume' (Hansen 1953, 35).

16.   Specifically, the automatic correction required would be a drop in interest rates sufficient
      to increase the production of capital goods such that adequate income levels would be
      restored. Since a poor community is more likely to consumer a larger percentage of its
      output, a smaller level of new investment would be required while a wealthier community
      will require larger levels of new investment to compensate for a wider gap between
      income and consumption. This problem is compounded by the fact that a wealthy
      community has less need for new investment since it already possesses a greater
      accumulation of capital (Keynes 1936, 31).

6. Contrasting economic outlooks and policy recommendations

No doubt we all agree that extremes of wealth and poverty are unjust –
especially when they do not correspond with personal effort or sacrifice –
and are bad in other ways.
The question is, what can we do about it?
Frank H. Knight (1951)

The system is not self-adjusting, and, without purposive direction, it is
incapable of translating our actual poverty into our potential plenty.
John M. Keynes (1934)

The conceptualized realities of Knight and Keynes indicate that both economists shared a common belief that the model of a perfectly competitive free market failed to provide adequate guidance for the real world. In particular, both Knight and Keynes concluded that a system of free market competition yielded an inequitable distribution of income and wealth, because of the existence of uncertainty. Despite the presence of uncertainty in the real world, prevailing models of perfect competition failed to recognize this fact within their analytical frameworks, a point both Knight and Keynes criticized. In order to correct for the weaknesses of applying a model of perfect competition to an imperfect world, both Knight and Keynes agreed that there is a role for the state to play in economic affairs. Knight's view of a world characterized by immutable, ergodicity, however, contrasts with the transmutable, nonergodic world of Keynes. Not only did their views of reality differ, but their general outlook toward economic life itself differed as well, with Knight maintaining a largely pessimistic and Keynes a largely optimistic view toward society's ability to handle 'the economic problem'. This contrast leads Knight and Keynes to disagree as to precisely what the role of the state should be.

KNIGHT'S PESSIMISM

Despite the fact that Frank Knight accepted a system of free markets as the most desirable means to greater efficiency, he maintained a lifelong uneasiness about its ability to support a social structure of personal rights and freedom, given that the problems the system attempted to address are inherently ethical ones. For Knight, it falls upon the state to assume a limited, negative role of maintaining a system of rules and order, so that the mechanism of free markets can function effectively. In developing his proposals for improving the effectiveness of an economy based upon *laissez-faire*, Knight relied on his understanding that 'from the standpoint of social policy, two questions are to be raised. From one point of view, "society" is a husbandman or "*wirtschaftender Mensch*," interested in getting its work done as well and as cheaply as possible ... ' (Knight 1921a, 368). Knight believed this question is best addressed through a process in which individuals assume the risks involved in bringing together the factors of production in hopes of producing an acceptable level of profit. Interestingly, Knight believed that on average this reward could be negative for society as a whole, with a decreasing number of entrepreneurs earning a positive profit, and an increasing number incurring a loss.

Knight then considers ' ... the second question raised [which] is whether it is really good for the individual, and hence for society which is the individual in the aggregate, to have the risks of industry assumed by the former even if he is willing to do it at a loss, on the average, to himself' (Knight 1921a, 368). This observation leads Knight to conclude that, given the inherent limitations of human intelligence and rationality, there should be *limits* placed on the degree to which individuals should be allowed to take chances or to assume risk. There are ' ... limitations [on] the economic view of social organization as a mechanism for satisfying human wants ... man's chief interest in life is after all to find life interesting, which is a very different thing from merely consuming a maximum amount of wealth' (Knight 1921a, 369). Given these limitations, Knight claims that economics is in turn itself limited in use as a scientific tool in understanding human behavior.

Knight also recognized that certain aspects of human nature conflicted with the notion of complete, unfettered freedom, an observation that proved to be the basis for his ethical questions. He expressed the concern that ' ... the principle of freedom...takes other values out of the field of social action ... [social or collective] agreement on terms of co-operation through discussion is hard and always threatens to become impossible, even to degenerate into a fight. The only agreement called for in market relations is acceptance of the one essentially negative ethical principle, that the units are not to prey upon one another through coercion or fraud' (Knight 1951c, 267). Knight considered such 'predatory activity' to be the primary moral problem of a *laissez-faire* economic philosophy (Knight 1921a, 182).

Knight, however, was not merely concerned about the possibility that individuals would *intentionally* prey upon one another. His greater concern was the possibility that action taken by well-meaning individuals engaged in free-market economic activity would *unknowingly and unintentionally* bring harm to other individuals or to society as a whole. Knight feared the possibility that 'goodness, good intentions and good people so commonly do harm instead of good because of failure to *understand* social and other conditions and the consequences of action' (Knight and Merriam 1945, 52). This concern regarding the ability of members of society to understand, either individually or collectively the consequences of their actions affected his opinions negatively regarding the role of the state in economic affairs.

Knight's concern that individuals might be unable to reach 'agreement', was complicated by his belief that certain aspects of human nature inherently within individual members of society had failed to evolve as society itself had done. Knight observed that 'it is clear that a crucial part of the world situation, this world crisis we hear so much about, is that human nature simply has not evolved in or by or for this kind of world, this kind of social environment – a world of large-scale, free, mobile, progressive, rationalistic, individualistic relationships' (Knight 1960, 55). It was Knight's belief that this lack of individual evolution in thinking brought about the tendency for members of society to disagree with one another. As a result, 'any social problem arises out of a combination of conflicting and harmonious interests of individuals. Men could not be free, or really human, until they felt unfree, until they consciously raised questions about their pattern of social life, based on custom and authority; and this questioning entails disagreement. It is disagreement which gives rise to social problems' (Knight and Merriam 1945, 74).

Knight observed significant weaknesses within a competitive market system brought about by a lack of intelligent, rational action exacerbated by the existence of uncertainty. Despite his ongoing skepticism, Knight's major concern was not merely to criticize the system, but to understand it fully enough to be able to address the weaknesses that he saw. During his lifetime, questions regarding the ability of modern society to endure[1] were common. Knight himself saw reason for concern, citing two recent world wars and the Great Depression as examples that a free society had significant room for improvement. Knight commented that 'the question on the knees of the gods today is whether people are acquiring or will acquire in time the capacity to think correctly enough to be able to maintain a free society without disintegration' (Knight 1960, 54). This concern over 'correct thinking' is interwoven with his lifelong preoccupation with the attainment and use of 'intelligence' by members of society.

Knight was willing and even eager to point out the weaknesses he observed within a system of *laissez-faire* in hopes of preserving the benefits of a free-market system. At the heart of his criticisms is the observation that 'the most serious limitations of the free-market economy, and major problems set by it, arise from the fact that it takes the "units," individuals, families, etc., as "given," which is entirely unrealistic ... the market is an agency of co-operation between such given units ... but in the distribution of economic resources atomistic motivation tends powerfully toward cumulatively increasing inequality' (Knight 1951c, 271). It was Knight's view that individuals, left totally free to pursue their own personal gain would inevitably do so at the expense of other members of society, as was previously implied by his observation that profit for some grew at the expense of losses for others. According to Knight, this created a situation in which the freedom of one individual encroached upon the freedoms of another, leaving him with grave concerns over the resulting ethical dilemma posed by *laissez-faire*.

At its core, Knight's ethical condemnation of a free-market economy lies in the potential inability of individuals to deal with uncertainty in an intelligent way, and the inefficiencies resulting from a misallocation of resources due to errors in judgement on the part of many economic agents. The success of certain agents and their resulting profits compounds the potential for an inequitable distribution of income. He did not criticize the existence of a moderate degree of inequity in the distribution of income, but he certainly took issue with the extreme inequities he believed a free-market economic system fostered. Knight contended that 'no doubt we all agree that extremes of wealth and poverty are unjust – especially when they do not correspond with personal effort or sacrifice – and are bad in other ways. The question is, what can we do about it?' (Knight 1951c, 272). Making matters worse still is the tendency for wealth to create wealth, for the owners of growing stocks of capital resources to use their accumulated wealth to create still more, at the expense of others not so endowed.

It was Knight's belief that 'uncertainty is one of the fundamental facts of life' (Knight 1921a, 347) and an inherent component of business and personal decision-making, brought about by the evolving and dynamic nature of a progressive society. While Knight never believed that uncertainty could be totally eradicated, he did nonetheless believe that it could be reduced to a 'manageable' proportion. To achieve this, Knight identified the existence of at least four alternatives. The first was to increase the knowledge of the future possessed by individuals. The most expedient mechanism for the attainment of this goal was through the use of 'scientific research and the accumulation and study of the necessary data' (Knight 1921a, 347). Still, this involves significant cost, both explicit and implicit, a fact recognized by Knight.

A second alternative identified by Knight was the 'clubbing of uncertainties through large-scale organization of various forms' (Knight 1921a, 347). Knight recognized, for example, that the accumulation of monopoly power in the hands of corporations could encourage economic progress. He suggested that '[monopoly] is both badly misunderstood and grossly exaggerated in the popular mind. Much monopoly in the technical meaning is not only inevitable in a free and progressive economy; it must be called positively good' (Knight 1948, 294). Knight believed that the primary advantage of monopoly power was its stimulation of progress and innovation. He remained cautious, however, citing the existence of monopoly power accumulated with the goal of increased profit at the expense of social good. Knight warned, ' ... it is a serious problem to differentiate between the good and the bad ... and to make and enforce regulations to secure the best possible balance' (Knight 1948, 294).

Knight also suggested that uncertainty could be reduced through two other less realistic and less desirable alternatives. The first, increased 'control over the future' would entail high costs in terms of financial and human resources as well as the loss of significant individual freedom through the high level of organization that would be required. Finally, Knight conceded that by 'slowing up the march of progress' uncertainty could be reduced (Knight 1921a, 347). Clearly this alternative would be repugnant to Knight, who regarded the dynamic nature of social development and progress to be worthy of protection and preservation.

In identifying these alternative approaches to reducing uncertainty, Knight remained unwavering in his view that 'the fundamental issue ... [is] the essential evil of uncertainty, how great it is and hence how much we can afford to sacrifice in other ways in order to reduce it' (Knight 1921a, 347). Knight's recognition that sacrifice is required in order to reduce uncertainty coincides with his view that all problems of life are economic and, accordingly, individuals must allocate scarce resources in such a way that the maximum quantity of wants are satisfied. Knight was aware that opportunity costs were incurred when individuals take the actions required to minimize uncertainty, whether those actions were the gathering of data, the conducting of analysis, or simply assuming the risk of a wild guess.

While Knight extended the presuppositions of classical economic theory through his clarification of what he viewed to be appropriate analytical techniques,[2] he remained convinced that uncertainty prevented the theoretical constructs of classical economics from being practically applicable to the real world. However, he accepted the idea that economics exists as a social science to facilitate the use of 'resources wisely in the achievement of *given* ends' (Knight 1922, 34) and believed that the use of economic theory was useful in society's efforts at achieving economic goals. Knight maintained a pessimistic view, nonetheless, because such a conception of economics requires the assumption of the intelligent, rational *economic man*. According to Knight, 'the economic man is the individual who obeys economic laws, which is merely to say that he obeys *some* laws of conduct, it being the task of the science to find out what the laws are. He is the *rational* man, the man who knows what he wants and orders his conduct intelligently with a view to getting it' (Knight 1922, 35). What provided Knight with the basis for his pessimistic view of the workability of socially desirable economic outcomes based upon the actions of a rational, economic man within a scientifically predictable and controllable economic world is his recognition that '*there is no such man*' (Knight 1922, 35).

As a result of Knight's contention that no such economic man exists, he believed economics must be redefined as a social science of conduct that examines 'conduct *in so far* as conduct is amenable to scientific treatment, in so far as it is controlled by definable conditions and can be reduced to law. But this, measured by the standard of natural science, is not very far. *There are no data* for a science of conduct ... ' (Knight 1922, 36). If Knight had been able to accept the proposition of a true *economic man* characterized by rationality and intelligence, perhaps the pessimism he maintained regarding the applicability of economic theory would have been avoided.

As it was, Knight's cynicism was compounded by his concern that this lack of rational intelligence was due in large part to the role played by religion in society. In particular, Knight believed that religion, especially organized religion, had impeded progress by maintaining resistance to the acceptance of new ways of thinking. It was previously established in Chapter 2 of this study that religion was gradually becoming supplanted by enlightened thinking in the late 1800s and early 1900s, at least within intellectual circles. Nonetheless, Knight's close association with conservative religion continued to be a major influence upon his thinking, albeit a negative one. He came to believe that 'the religious ideal of the intellectual life is the conditioning of children in infancy to the unquestioning acceptance of dogma, myth and authority, and of the sinfulness of all criticism or questioning' (Knight and Merriam 1945, 41). In Knight's mind, the static nature of religion grew increasingly obsolete in a world of dynamic change. He contended 'the concrete working principle of original Christian social morality is not so much love as obedience; established custom, law and authority are to be accepted as the will of God' (Knight and Merriam 1945, 36).

While Knight appears to admire the message of a universal brotherhood characterized by tolerance and love, he remains concerned that the romantic thinking brought about by such teaching impairs the ability of individuals to make intelligent, objective decisions. Knight believed 'the greater danger from Christian ethics lies in the tendency to carry the sentimental, brotherhood morality of primitive tribal life – more especially the condemnation of differences in wealth and power, which are organizational conditions of efficiency – into practical measures of internal social reform to such an extent, or in such ways, as to work serious injury' (Knight and Merriam 1945, 95). Knight, therefore, recognizes the role played by 'differences in wealth and power' in motivating the actions of members of society, deeming it a necessary evil for a market system to possess in order to achieve its goal of efficient resource allocation. He nonetheless remained an intense critic of the arbitrary nature of income and wealth distribution as the result of the success or failure of individuals to make rational and intelligent decisions in the face of uncertainty.

KEYNES' OPTIMISM

While Knight's pessimism often resulted in a decidedly cynical perspective on society's ability to work out its economic problems, Keynes adopted a more optimistic tone. Whereas Knight failed to define a long-term vision of the future, Keynes looked past the economic problems of his day with an eye toward an improved future. Despite his proclamation that in the long-run individuals who are struggling with the economic problems of the day would all be 'dead', and despite his emphasis on short-term analysis, he nonetheless looked to the distant future with an attitude of positive expectation.

Keynes looked optimistically into the future, proclaiming ' ... the day is not far off when the economic problem will take the back seat where it belongs, and that the arena of the heart and head will be occupied, or re-occupied, by our real problems – the problems of life and of human relations, of creation and behavior and religion' (Keynes 1931, vii). The context of Keynes' comments is important to understand. His preface to 'Essays in Persuasion' reflects his feeling that, at the time (1931), European society in general, and Britain in particular was 'at a point of transition'. Many of the essays contained in the volume pertained to his feelings toward what he viewed as 'the three great controversies of the past decade ... the Treaty of Peace and the War Debts, the Policy of Deflation, and the Return to the Gold Standard ... ' (Keynes 1930b, vi). Likewise, Keynes was among other writers of his day who were responding to the growing threat of Communism and the economic alternative it provided. Nonetheless, the collection of essays within the volume reflects Keynes' concern over contemporary economic problems and also his more philosophical views about a positive, albeit distant, future.

Keynes, did not, however, make these proclamations in a merely anecdotal way. He applied his understanding of contemporary matters to questions of future economic development and arrived at his forecast in a methodical, logical manner. Nevertheless, he was discouraged by the existence of ' ... a bad attack of economic pessimism ... ' (Keynes 1930b, 358) that he believed was plaguing society in 1930, when he wrote his optimistic foretelling 'Economic Possibilities for our Grandchildren'. While admitting that society was in the midst of ' ... growing-pains of over-rapid changes, from the painfulness of readjustment between one economic period and another ... [with] ... the increase of technical efficiency ... taking place faster than we can deal with the problem of labour absorption ... [and] ... the improvement in the standard of life ... [being] ... a little too quick ... [while] ... the banking and monetary system of the world ... [prevents] the rate of interest from falling as fast as equilibrium requires ... ', he nonetheless believed that the 'errors of pessimism which now make so much noise in the world will be proved wrong in our own time' (Keynes 1930b, 358–9).

Keynes suggested that the modern era can trace its beginning to the sixteenth century when capital accumulation began to occur in earnest for the first time. It was Keynes' opinion that this accumulation of capital, combined with the acceleration of technical innovation throughout the following centuries, allowed society to significantly improve its standard of living, despite rapid worldwide growth in population (Keynes 1930b, 363). By applying a rate of growth based upon historical trends to existing capital stocks, Keynes supposes that ' ... a hundred years hence we are all of us, on the average, eight times better off in the economic sense than we are to-day' (Keynes 1930b, 365). This projection allows Keynes to conclude that ' ... assuming no important wars and no important increase in population, the *economic problem* may be solved, or be at least within sight of solution, within a hundred years'. The most important implication of this statement is that '...the economic problem is not – if we look into the future – *the permanent problem of the human race*' (Keynes 1930b, 365–6).

This optimistic long-run outlook did not stop Keynes from recognizing problems in present-day economic affairs, particularly ethical problems. He abhorred the pursuit of money and profit for its own sake and recognized this as the root of society's ethical and moral problems. The result of 'capitalistic individualism', thought Keynes, was unemployment. Still, capitalism was associated with certain attributes thought to be desirable by society, namely efficiency and freedom. Keynes sought to perpetuate the efficiency and freedom of capitalism while applying the ' ... right analysis of the problem to cure the disease...' (Keynes 1936, 381).

Despite his ethical criticism of capitalism, Keynes was willing to admit the role played by the profit-seeking capitalists in economic development. 'The strenuous purposeful money-makers may carry all of us along with them into the lap of economic abundance'. Other members of society will benefit positively, including those people 'who can keep alive, and cultivate into a fuller perfection, the art of life itself and do not sell themselves for the means of life, who will be able to enjoy the abundance when it comes' (Keynes 1930b, 368). Still, Keynes looked forward to the day when 'the love of money as a possession – as distinguished from the love of money as a means to the enjoyments and realities of life – will be recognised for what it is, a somewhat disgusting morbidity, one of those semi-criminal, semi-pathological propensities which one hands over with a shudder to the specialists in mental disease' (Keynes 1930b, 369).

At the core of Keynes' criticisms of money-loving behavior is his conviction that for outcomes to be 'good' economic actors were required *themselves to be good*. A world in which the future is uncertain complicates the efforts of individual's to be and do good, especially when the 'good' is defined in terms of what is socially desirable. The incorporation of uncertainty as a primary point of divergence between Keynes' economic theory and classical economic theory therefore provides Keynes with impetus for his philosophical and ethical considerations.

Specifically, whereas Keynes denied the existence of 'rationality' in the sense that individuals possess perfect and complete knowledge of the present and the future, he did not deny a rationality in which individuals possess ' … the right reason even if the answer is wrong' (Fitzgibbons 1991, 131). The existence of uncertainty in Keynes' models forced him to incorporate an assumption of rationality different from that of the 'rational economic man'. Keynes' ethically-based conception of rationality was one in which individuals most often consider the consequences of their actions before taking such action. (Fitzgibbons 1991, 131).

It was this recognition of present-day moral and ethical problems that forced Keynes to admit that the economic problems facing his society must still be addressed with assertive policy action. Keynes was painfully aware that the days in which 'avarice is a vice, that the exaction of usury is a misdemeanour, and the love of money is detestable, that those walk most truly in the paths of virtue and sane widom who take least thought for the morrow … [and when] we shall once more value ends above means' (Keynes 1930b, 371–2) were still to come. He cautioned his readers to beware, proclaiming that for another one hundred years to come, the actions of others must be viewed with suspicion and caution. This is so because 'avarice and usury and precaution must be our gods for a little longer still. For only they can lead us out of the tunnel of economic necessity into daylight' (Keynes 1930b, 372).

Like Knight, Keynes stopped short of outright condemnation of *laissez-faire* and the capitalist system of political economy that *laissez-faire* had promulgated. The focus of Keynes' work became directed toward developing a set of remedies to correct for insufficient effective demand and the resulting high levels of involuntary unemployment. It was his hope that his long-term vision of freedom from economic concerns could be reached through the preservation of a free-market system guided by purposeful collective action. Keynes believed it essential that population growth be controlled, that war be avoided, that science be applied only to those areas in which science is truly applicable, and that the growth and accumulation of wealth should be tied to the relationship that exists between production and consumption (Keynes 1930b, 373).

Most important, it was Keynes' opinion that in order for society to arrive at the optimistic future he envisioned, one must maintain a positive outlook. More than that, Keynes recognized a role to be played by faith, a linchpin of theological and religious values, in attaining desired economic and social ends. According to Keynes, ' … it happens that there is a subtle reason drawn from economic analysis why, in this case, faith may work. For if we consistently act on the optimistic hypothesis, this hypothesis will tend to be realised; whilst by acting on the pessimistic hypothesis we can keep ourselves for ever in the pit of want' (Keynes 1931, viii). The suggestion that 'faith may work' is a revealing indication of the fundamental role played by uncertainty in the thinking of Keynes. After all, in a world of *certainty* faith would not be required.

THEORETICAL SUPREMACY OF THE FREE MARKET

Despite Knight's insistent concerns that an economy characterized by *laissez-faire* is unjust in its distribution of income shares, he nonetheless observed that a free-market economy possessed certain notable positive aspects, in particular a system of free exchange. He believed 'the supreme and inestimable merit of the exchange mechanism is that it enables a vast number of people to co-operate in the use of means to achieve ends as far as their interests are mutual, without arguing or in any way agreeing about either the ends or the methods of achieving them' (Knight 1951c, 267). This view of the free market suggests that its role is more than one of commerce, it is also one of providing social order and organization. This is Knight's predominant, conservative view, but one that created in him an ethical dilemma.

To facilitate his analysis Knight equated economic activity to participation in a well-organized game. Knight observed that 'while men are "playing the game" of business, they are also moulding their own and other personalities, and creating a civilization whose worthiness to endure cannot be a matter of indifference' (Knight 1923, 47). Knight's ethical question, therefore, was ' ... *what kind of game is business?'* (Knight 1923, 46).

Knight answers his own question by suggesting that a policy of *laissez-faire*, built upon the fundamental element of individualism is applicable in its true form only to conditions of pure competition, a condition that is non-existent in the real world. Knight recognized that ' ... one of the most important prerequisites to perfect competition is complete knowledge on the part of every competing individual of the exchange opportunities open to him ... ' (Knight 1923, 51). This lack of perfect knowledge forces players of the economic game to resort to the application of statistical analysis based upon past results, present conditions, and future expectations. In some cases, the imperfect knowledge becomes transformed into probabilistic 'risk', while in other cases 'uncertainty' remains. It is the existence of risk and uncertainty, however, that contributes to making the game worth playing. According to Knight 'all human planning and execution involve uncertainty, and a rational social order can be realized through individual action only if all persons have a rational attitude toward risk and chance' (Knight 1923, 54). Knight maintained the opinion that this simply was not the case, concluding that collective action is required to maintain such a 'rational social order'.

Knight adheres to the conservative view that individual freedom is best preserved through a system of free markets, rather than centralized control. Knight nonetheless recognized the inherent weaknesses of a free-market economic system when he considered the question of whether it provides three fundamental components required of a 'good competitive game'. Namely, it is necessary that its participants have the ability to play, that the game 'test the capacity of the players' and therefore requires the exertion of effort, and finally that the results of the game 'be unpredictable: if there is no element of luck in it there is no game' (Knight 1923, 63).

It was Knight's observation that the free-market economies of the real world possessed significant shortcomings including the fact that 'the terms on which different individuals enter the contest are too unequal' and the element of luck is so great that 'capacity and effort' often 'count for nothing' (Knight 1923, 64). This problem becomes particularly acute for the 'propertyless and ill-paid masses' who protest against 'a low scale of living' and 'against the terms of what they feel to be an unfair contest in which being defeated by the stacking of the cards against them is perhaps as important to their feelings as the physical significance of the stakes which they lose' (Knight 1923, 60).

Nonetheless, Knight viewed the development of *laissez-faire*, and its concomitant value of freedom positively from a historical perspective, noting that 'the establishment of freedom ... is the greatest revolution of all time or since the dawn of conscious life' (Knight 1951c, 289). Knight believed that freedom of all sorts, including free enterprise, led to 'the most rapid advance yet seen … in humanitarianism, the unification of the world's peoples, and the diffusion of the advantages of civilized life among the populations of the advanced nations, and among others as fast as they were able to join in the movement' (Knight 1948, 289). Knight therefore believes that, while imperfect, the free-market system brings about the highest possible level of efficiency and progress.

Nevertheless, according to Knight, 'the statement that under perfect competition the free-enterprise organization of economic life would achieve for everyone the best combination of freedom and efficiency does not at all imply either that the actual system is ethically ideal or that nothing can be done to improve it' (Knight and Merriam 1945, 105). But Knight believed that the problems attributed to *laissez-faire*, such as income inequity, the growth of monopoly power, and unemployment, existed not because of a weakness in orthodox economic theory itself but in the fact that the real world has little in common with the assumed reality of pure competition. This discrepancy between theory and reality is especially obvious given the fact that the real world is characterized by less than perfect knowledge – or uncertainty. Uncertainty itself has positive and negative aspects, on the one hand creating the opportunity for profit, on the other creating potential for losses.

This dichotomy of ends is due to Knight's belief that individuals are often influenced by 'romantic' thinking, which frequently results in irrational decision making. As a result, Knight held that economic theory should not be overly relied upon to establish policy for a world of imperfectly competitive markets, but that the application of theory was nonetheless *useful* in understanding the workings of a free market economy, as long as the weaknesses of such theory were kept in mind (Knight 1924, 235). In particular, Knight accepted the proposition that classical economic theory, called 'classical liberalism' by Knight, was the theory best suited to serve an economy characterized by individualism and evolutionary progress.

In Knight's view, classical theory provided the best mechanism for explaining the creation and accumulation of profit. In spite of his claim that the theoretical assumptions of classical economic theory do not necessarily coincide with real world conditions, Knight nonetheless believed that the use of such theory and its resulting quantitative models in understanding the economy was appropriate, as long as the shortcomings were understood. Knight viewed the major shortcoming of the classical theory of perfect competition to be its failure in assuming perfect knowledge, rather than uncertainty. Hence, Knight was able to accept the 'mechanics' of classical theory, while recognizing that the creation and accumulation of profit was the result of market imperfections, namely the existence of 'true uncertainty'.

This 'true uncertainty' prevents the 'theoretically perfect outworking of the tendencies of competition [and] gives the characteristic form of "enterprise" to economic organization as a whole and accounts for the peculiar income of the entrepreneur' (Knight 1921a, 232).

Given Knight's acceptance of classical (or neoclassical) economic theory, it remained for him to reconcile his ethical concerns regarding the problems inherent within a system of unregulated and uncontrolled markets with the benefits of an individualistic, utilitarian society. His solution is a compromising middle way in which he assigns to the government certain regulatory roles intended to assure a smooth operation to a system of otherwise free markets.[3] Knight believed that if property rights were clearly assigned and if a well understood system of rules were in place, then the operation of a free-market economy could be conducted with many of its inherent problems lessened in severity. Knight observed that 'an economic system of "free" market relations, even in its maximum development, must operate in a framework of political order, to protect property and enforce the rules of the market' (Knight 1934, 288).[4]

Democratic Political Guidance

Knight embraces the efficiencies and therefore the economic advantages of a free-market economy but he also believes the government had a role, albeit a limited one, in regulating the affairs of society. He takes a moderate stance, saying 'democracy faces the hard problem of a proper division of functions between government and other forms of association, and policy needs to lean toward the more voluntary' (Knight 1960, 35). He continues, 'actually, the issue is never economics or politics; it is always a question of the best combination – not only of the best proportion, but also of the best way to integrate the tendencies of the free market system with political action' (Knight 1960, 111).

Recall that Knight's concerns regarding the ability of individuals rationally and intelligently to arrive at socially optimal decisions led him to have grave ethical concerns about *laissez-faire*. In Knight's opinion, given the fact that many individuals lacked the necessary knowledge and rationality to make objective decisions based on available information, he feared that society, in turn, would lack the same traits. It therefore becomes necessary for a free-market economy to rely on outside forces, namely the State, to assist the market in reaching its goals. Knight was concerned that ' ... the business organizations which are the directing divinities of the system are but groups of ignorant and frail beings like the individuals with whom they deal ... the system as a whole is dependent upon an outside organization, an authoritarian state, made up also of ignorant and frail human beings, to provide a setting in which it can operate at all' (Knight 1924, 236).

Knight therefore recognized the role played by the State in providing a hospitable social environment in which the business of life could occur but remained skeptical, fearing that a government composed of 'ignorant' individuals would itself remain 'ignorant'. Nonetheless, Knight identified other roles to be assumed by the State. Specifically, Knight believed it to be acceptable for the government to 'define and protect property rights, enforce contract and prevent non-contractual (compulsory) transactions, maintain a circulating medium, and most especially prevent that collusion and monopoly, the antithesis of competition, into which competitive relations constantly tend to gravitate' (Knight 1924, 236). Knight believed that a wisely-led government would be able to carry out these tasks, ensuring a more smoothly operating system of free markets and, in turn, preserving the freedom and individuality so cherished by members of modern society.

All the same, Knight maintained some degree of concern that there could be such a thing as wisely-led government, nonetheless maintaining that 'an economic system of "free" market relations, even in its maximum development, must operate in a framework of political order, to protect property and enforce the rules of the market' (Knight 1934, 288). Like Keynes, Knight was highly critical of the authoritative governments rising to power in the early part of the twentieth century, but took a much more conservative stance than Keynes in advocating policy that reinforced the supremacy of uncontrolled free markets. His writing reflects his plea for the preservation of *democracy*. Knight believed that when the 'economic game' reaches the stage of development in which 'the growth of individual inequality and monopoly' become problems for society, it falls to the state to provide a remedy (Knight 1934, 293).

Improvements to Education

Knight's hope that the State could somehow provide order to otherwise free markets resulted in another significant recommendation. In order to ensure the existence of a competent government made up of intelligent individuals, Knight proposed improvements to the educational system. He believed that the way to a more rational, intelligent political leadership was to 'raise the general level of public intelligence; to raise their own [political leaders, economists, and others] level through research and critical thinking; to train specialists for active and co-operative participation in the political process; and to inculcate a right attitude of mutual understanding and respect in the public ... ' (Knight 1944a, 334). Without expressly saying so, Knight appeared to lean toward the church's minimizing its participation in the educational process, preferring it to be undertaken by more objective organizations. Knight believed that 'the first test of a free society is that it teach its youth to question and criticize and form opinion only by weighing evidence – and to admit ignorance where there is no evidence – instead of implanting eternal and immutable truth ... ' (Knight 1951c, 274–5). In Knight's opinion, reaching this goal is made more difficult because organized religion exerts significant control over maintaining ethical tradition and opinion through education. 'In fact', remarked Knight, 'I see as the main task of general education to "unteach," to overcome the prejudice and the inclination to snap judgments and develop the will to be intelligent, i.e., objective and critical' (Knight 1960, 4).

FAILURE OF THE FREE MARKET

It has been established that Keynes viewed the most significant failure of a free-market economy to be its inability to 'provide for full employment and its arbitrary and inequitable distribution of wealth and incomes' (Keynes 1936, 372). Keynes traced this failure to the fact of uncertainty. It was Keynes' observation that classical economic theory was based upon the assumption that the Benthamite calculus of pleasure and pain influenced the ethical behavior of individuals. Unfortunately, individuals often fail to consider anything other than the immediate consequences of their actions. Among the more remote consequences, Keynes believed, was the uneven distribution of accumulated wealth that frequently plagued industrial society. Since the accumulation of wealth is associated with a sometimes distant and uncertain future, the application of classical economic theory is particularly inappropriate. The actions of individuals simply do not always reflect the objective calculation of rational individuals in determining the best course of action.

Nonetheless, despite the fact of an uncertain future, according to Keynes, '... the necessity for action and for decision compels us as practical men to do our best to overlook this awkward fact and to behave exactly as we should if we had behind us a good Benthamite calculation of a series of prospective advantages and disadvantages, each multiplied by its appropriate probability, waiting to be summed' (Keynes 1937a, 214). Decisions must be made in the face of an uncertain future, and are usually based upon mere opinion or 'animal spirits'. While individuals may not *actually* be rational economic men, they *pretend* to be, making and justifying decisions *as if* the tools of Benthamite calculus are at their disposal.

According to Keynes, this feat 'saves our faces as rational men' (Keynes 1937a, 214) and is accomplished by 1) assuming that 'the present is a much more serviceable guide to the future than a candid examination of past experience would show it to have been hitherto ... '; 2) assuming that the existing level of prices and output is based upon a correct estimation of 'future prospects'; 3) resorting to the 'judgment of the rest of the world which is perhaps better informed' (Keynes 1937a, 214). Probability serves as a *tool* in this effort, in that Keynes believed it to be *rational* for individuals to use statistical analysis as a *guide* in their decision making (Keynes 1921, 323). Unfortunately, this constitutes a 'flimsy foundation' upon which to base future expectations and, as a result, society falls victim to ' ... sudden and violent changes' in economic conditions (Keynes 1937a, 214–15). The weakness of probability analysis is that its application does not guarantee certainty of outcomes, merely an indication of what a given outcome *might* be.

Given Keynes' view that uncertainty is unavoidable, it should come as no surprise that he regarded the tendency for individuals to possess a liquidity preference as a hedge against uncertainty, uncertainty as to the future rate of interest in particular, as inevitable. The ramification of such a liquidity preference upon effective demand is significant, yet unforeseen by the articulators of classical economic theory who continued to call for a *laissez-faire* policy, allowing the natural order of self-interest and competition to work out the problems prevalent within a modern economic system.

Keynes was more optimistic than Knight regarding the ability of individuals to work collectively in addressing economic problems. Rather than accept the proposition that the natural economic order should be allowed to carry society along some predetermined path toward long-term economic Utopia, Keynes believed purposeful human action was required for this outcome to be achieved. This emphasis upon policy action stands as one of the most outstanding features of 'Keynes the economist' (Landreth and Colander 1994, 461).

Keynes' *magnum opus*, *The General Theory*, contains considerable detail regarding specific policy recommendations.[5] While his writing on this subject has been the subject of much debate and interpretation, there does appear to be general agreement that Keynes himself recognized the important role that the State could play in promoting economic stability in the face of the problems inherent in a free-market economy. Keynes stated clearly that his *General Theory* 'indicates the vital importance of establishing certain central controls in matters which are now left in the main to individual initiative' (Keynes 1936, 377). Specifically, Keynes saw a role for 'central controls' in influencing the level of aggregate spending, but 'apart from the necessity of central controls to bring about an adjustment ... [in aggregate spending] ... there is no need to socialize economic life than there was before' (Keynes 1936, 379).

The major problem to be addressed was not in a misallocation of workers (or resources) but in the volume of such resources employed. Keynes noted that 'the complaint against the present system ... is in determining the volume, not the direction, of actual employment'; it is here that 'the existing system has broken down' (Keynes 1936, 379). Such involuntary unemployment stems from insufficient effective demand, disappointing the expectations of businesses. As has been established, Keynes identified the causes of such insufficient effective demand as being the 'fundamental psychological law' – the marginal propensity to consume, and the rate of new investment. In order to compensate, Keynes proposed a large and influential role for the government to play in economic affairs. Among the policy recommendations mentioned by Keynes (and extended by his followers), his suggestions that investment be 'socialized', and that the government assume a more active role through deficit spending are of particular relevance to this study, given that these recommendations contain especially important social and ethical ramifications.

Socialization of Investment

Classical theory had assumed that higher interest rates were required to stimulate savings. Keynes noted that, in fact, the level of savings is related to the level of investment and that in order for investment to occur, interest rates had to be low. According to Keynes, ' ... it is to our best advantage to reduce the rate of interest to that point relatively to the schedule of the marginal efficiency of capital at which there is full employment' (Keynes 1936, 375). Keynes was doubtful that 'the influence of banking policy on the rate of interest will be sufficient by itself to determine an optimum rate of investment' (Keynes 1936, 378). Keynes' most important and controversial policy recommendation became his call for a 'somewhat comprehensive socialization of investment' which Keynes believed would 'prove the only means of securing an approximation of full employment' (Keynes 1936, 378).

Keynes believed that the State would be required to assume an active role in this endeavor since ' ... I am now somewhat sceptical of the success of a merely monetary policy directed toward influencing the rate of interest'. Because of the existence of uncertainty and ' ... the effects of our ignorance of the future ... ', it was Keynes' opinion that ' ... I expect to see the State, which is in a position to calculate the marginal efficiency of capital-goods on long views and on the basis of the general social advantage, taking an ever greater responsibility for directly organising investment ... ' (Keynes 1936, 163–4). The State, in Keynes' opinion, is capable of achieving and maintaining a longer-term perspective than the typical individual investor.

This 'long-view' allows investment to occur that is not merely undertaken with the motive of short-term profit. In achieving this goal, the ' … aggregate return from durable goods in the course of their life would, as in the case of short-lived goods, just cover their labour-costs of production *plus* an allowance for risk and the costs of skill and supervision' (Keynes 1936, 375).

Recognizing that the suggestion of socialized investment would be a controversial one, conflicting with the established value of personal freedom, Keynes explains further that his recommendation is ' … quite compatible with some measure of individualism … ' (Keynes 1936, 375). Nonetheless, Keynes considered this proposal to be a mechanism not only through which investment could be raised to a higher level, but also a way in which capitalism could rid itself of one of its greatest evils, the ' … cumulative oppressive power of the capitalist to exploit the scarcity-value of capital' for it is through the 'agency of the state' that 'communal saving' can be maintained at the level necessary to ' … allow the growth of capital up to the point where it ceases to become scarce' (Keynes 1936, 376). It was Keynes' opinion that the socialization of investment would bring about the 'euthanasia of the rentier', an economic actor whose purpose would have been served during a ' … transitional phase … ' and who would ' … disappear when it has done its work' (Keynes 1936, 376).

The ultimate goal of such a policy would be to ' … aim in practice … at an increase in the volume of capital until it ceases to be scarce, so that the functionless investor will no longer receive a bonus; and at a scheme of direct taxation which allows the intelligence and determination and executive skill of the financier, the entrepreneur … to be harnessed to the service of the community on reasonable terms of reward' (Keynes 1936, 376–7).

Despite his aggressive proposal for reform, Keynes was conscience of public sentiment regarding freedom and the rights of the individual in relation to economic matters. The ethical implication of proposing collective action to replace individual decision-making is profound. Keynes was quick, however, to present his proposal as part of society's long-term evolution, rather than short-term revolution. 'It will be … that the euthanasia of the rentier, of the functionless investor, will be nothing sudden, merely a gradual but prolonged continuance … and will need no revolution' (Keynes 1936, 376). The process of socialization 'can be introduced gradually and without a break in the general traditions of society' (Keynes 1936, 378).

Likewise, Keynes was quick to point out the fact that his proposal in no way recommended overall socialization of economic activity. While he advocated central control over specific areas of economic life presently in the hands of the private sector, he advocated little other change. 'The State will have to exercise a guiding influence on the propensity to consume partly through its scheme of taxation, partly by fixing the rate of interest, and partly, perhaps, in other ways' (Keynes 1936, 378). Keynes believed that only through 'a somewhat comprehensive socialization of investment' would society reach the goal of full employment.

Keynes was therefore very aware of the possible reaction to such proposals, claiming that ' ... it is rash to predict how the average man will react to a changed environment ... and it would remain for separate decision on what scale and by what means it is right and reasonable to call on the living generation to restrict their consumption, so as to establish, in course of time, a state of full investment for their successors' (Keynes 1936, 377). Keynes saw no reason to call for any sort of comprehensive State Socialism, believing that the ownership of capital must remain in the hands of the private sector and that the State would merely determine the socially optimal level of investment within various sectors as well as the interest rate rewarded to the owners of capital because ' ... I see no reason to suppose that the existing system seriously misemploys the factors of production ... ' (Keynes 1936, 378–9).

Expansionary Fiscal Policy

Keynes recognized that there were limits to the effectiveness of monetary policy. Specifically, he believed that there existed a *liquidity trap* that existed at points in which interest rates had been pushed to very low levels. After interest rates have fallen to a very low level, ' ... liquidity-preference may become virtually absolute in the sense that almost everyone prefers cash to holding a debt which yields so low a rate of interest'. At this point, according to Keynes, the 'monetary authority would have lost effective control over the rate of interest' (Keynes 1936, 207). Keynes did not concern himself much with this prospect, since he had not observed such a situation having existed in the past. Even if it came to be, he realized that the State would then be able to borrow extensively at low interest rates in order to use deficit spending to increase effective demand. His recognition that monetary policy alone might not be sufficient to allow an economic system to recover from economic downturns therefore led Keynes to consider the possibility of fiscal policy to reach the same goal.

Given Keynes' belief in the relative stability of the propensity to consume, such that the level of aggregate consumption is largely dependent upon aggregate income, it becomes especially critical to maintain employment at a satisfactorily high level for incomes in turn to be adequate to assure sufficient effective demand. The seemingly circular nature of this dilemma led Keynes to admit the importance of fiscal policy. In some cases, fiscal policy might take effect simply because the ' ... decline in income due to a decline in the level of employment, if it goes far, may even cause consumption to exceed income not only by some individuals and institutions using up the financial reserves which they have accumulated in better times, but also by the Government, which will be liable, willingly or unwillingly, to run into a budgetary deficit or will provide unemployment relief, for example, out of borrowed money' (Keynes 1936, 98). It would appear that Keynes recognized the fact that there is some minimum level of consumption that must occur, even at very low levels of income. This 'subsistence' level, as it might be called could very well become the responsibility of the government to provide.

It is frequently suggested that Keynes advocated the running of budget deficits, in order to pull an economy out of depression. While Keynes perhaps left room for such interpretation, it may by that Keynes actually advocated the use of public borrowing or 'loan expenditure' for certain types of public investment and expenditure. Yet he was precise in his thinking that certain types of public expenditure would better serve the people than others. Under conditions of involuntary employment, for example, it would be better to incur budget deficits in order to provide a system of public works programs, putting the unemployed to work, rather than simply providing unemployment relief payments (Keynes 1936, 128).

Keynes obviously opposed the concept of unemployment compensation or welfare entitlements, suggesting that society would be better served if ' ... the Treasury were to fill old bottles with banknotes, bury them at suitable depths in disused coal mines which are then filled up to the surface with town rubbish, and leave it to private enterprise on well-tried principles of *laissez-faire* to dig the notes up again ... '. As a result, ' ... there need be no more unemployment and, with the help of the repercussions, the real income of the community, and its capital wealth also, would probably become a good deal greater than it actually is' (Keynes 1936, 129). The use of public works programs, financed by public borrowing, would in all likelihood increase employment and income. When combined with the effect of the multiplier, the ultimate benefit to society would be much greater than the initial expenditure.

The Middle Way

Despite his call for purposeful collective action by the State, Keynes nonetheless remained a supporter of a system of entrepreneurially driven markets, given the resulting benefits of such a system. It was Keynes' intention to 'indicate the nature of the environment which the free play of economic forces requires if it is to realise the full potentialities of production' (Keynes 1936, 379). Keynes especially admired the efficiency of free enterprise and the concomitant advantages of decentralization and social progress that came from the allocation of resources brought on by the profit-seeking endeavors of corporate and individual economic activity. According to Keynes, ' … no case is made for State socialism which would embrace most of the economic life of the community' (Keynes 1936, 378).

Indeed, Keynes recognized that ' … above all, individualism, if it can be purged of its defects and its abuses, is the best safeguard of personal liberty in the sense that, compared with any other system, it greatly widens the field for the exercise of personal choice' (Keynes 1936, 380). Doubtlessly, Keynes believed the most significant 'defect' of individualism to be the highly inequitable distribution of income and wealth brought about by its greatest 'abuse', an insatiable hunger for profit and personal gain. Still, Keynes observed that an economic system of free markets allowed individuals to exercise their much-valued freedom of choice, a right that he saw rapidly disappearing in the totalitarian dictatorships of Germany, Italy, and Russia.

It was therefore not the goal of Keynes to obliterate the social and economic structure that existed at the time of his writing. Rather, he sought a compromising, albeit aggressive, role for the State to play in stabilizing the modern, real-world economic system in which society lived.[6] Still, Keynes believed that the system of free enterprise, as analyzed via classical economic precepts, functioned adequately in regard to ' … the manner in which private self-interest will determine what in particular is produced, in what proportions the factors of production will be combined to produce it, and how the value of the final product will be distributed between them' (Keynes 1936, 378–9).

Nonetheless, the problem of deficient effective demand brought about a 'public scandal of wasted resources' and results in a situation in which the individual entrepreneur, who, in an attempt to conduct business in such an environment, ' … is operating with the odds loaded against him' (Keynes 1936, 381). Keynes believed that industrious people often incur financial losses because of a shortfall in effective demand, despite the possession of 'average skill and average good fortune'. Given an adequate level of effective demand, these losses can be erased and greater social progress could occur.

Keynes advocated a 'middle way' for the State to provide a stabilizing, rather than an authoritarian role in promoting economic stability. Specifically, rather than relying on export-led growth, the State's primary goals must be ' … involved in the task of adjusting to one another the propensity to consume and the inducement to invest … ' (Keynes 1936, 380). Using the mechanisms of monetary policy to affect the level of investment by reducing the rate of interest or by influencing the propensity to consume through fiscal policy, Keynes believed that this role for the State was ' … the only practicable means of avoiding the destruction of existing economic forms in their entirety and as the condition of the successful functioning of individual motive'. He denied any contention that his proposals were ' ... a terrific encroachment on individualism' (Keynes 1936, 380).

Above all, Keynes believed the favorable benefits associated with individual freedoms and choice must be preserved. Keynes' optimistic outlook and faith in the ability of individuals to behave as though they were rational, allowed him to maintain the view that society would ultimately solve its economic problem. Keynes was able to see past the problems of scarcity, unemployment, and poverty, and proposed ways in which individualism, personal choice, and the resulting 'variety of life' could be preserved and extended. Keynes believed ' ... this variety preserves the traditions which embody the most secure and successful choices of former generations; it colours the present with the diversification of its fancy; and, being the handmaid of experiment as well as of tradition and of fancy, it is the most powerful instrument to better the future' (Keynes 1936, 380).

While more supportive than Keynes of classical liberalism as the body of theory to be applied to general economic questions, Knight clearly remained skeptical of its practical application to a real world of imperfect competition. Knight's allowance for the fact of uncertainty and its resulting effect on the efficient resource allocation and distribution of income shares reflects his belief that the prevailing theory must be made to accommodate the facts of the real world. As a result, a free-market economy, while resulting in some significant benefits to society, nonetheless results in frequent inequities brought about by the individualistic utilitarian behavior of irrational economic agents.

Knight's 'middle way' limits his suggestions for State involvement to merely providing a framework of rules and laws in which the game of economic life may be played. His equating of economic life with a game is readily apparent in his descriptions of a freely competitive organization of society in which society tends 'to place every productive resource in that position ... where it can make the greatest possible addition to the total social dividend...and tends to reward every participant in production by giving it the increase in the social dividend which its co-operation makes possible' (Knight 1923, 58). The imagery of a game is unmistakable, yet Knight questioned the fairness of such a game in the presence of extreme inequities that result from it being played by sometimes unintelligent and irrational players.

While skeptical of the intelligence and rationality of individuals within economic society, Knight nonetheless appears to have believed that collectively, there is hope for some degree of rational action. Knight regarded the critics of free-market economies with the same sort of skepticism regarding their own intelligence. He believed that 'radical critics of competition as a general basis of the economic order generally underestimate egregiously the danger of doing vastly worse' (Knight 1923, 58).

In coming to this conclusion, Knight regarded the role of the State as that of an umpire or referee in the great economic game. Rather than purposefully affecting the outcome, the State merely ensures that the players obey the rules of the game as they exercise their own rights and freedoms in pursuit of their own individual interests, while recognizing the rights of others to do the same. According to Knight, the organization of these activities is best left to a system of free markets, in which the State plays a facilitating role.

Knight believed that economics dealt with the social organization of economic activity (Knight 1951a, 6). Since economics deals with society, it becomes subject to much interpretation and differences of opinion as to what form the structure of economic organization should take. According to Knight, 'economic and other activities will always be organized in all the possible ways, and the problem is to find the right proportions between individualism and socialism and the various varieties of each, and to use each in its proper place' (Knight 1923, 58).

NOTES

1. In particular, the rise of totalitarian power in Italy, Japan, and Germany and the problems brought about by growing extremes of economic fluctuation became of increasing concern.
2. Such as the use of the theoretical model of perfect competition, including utility theory, even though conditions of the real world prevented it from being applied without error. Knight simultaneously observed that the tendency of pure competition is toward monopoly and other market imperfections.
3. Knight indicated his belief at one point that a 'drastic system of taxation', rather than 'most proposals for social interference in contractual relations' would be the most likely and most direct way in which to achieve greater income equality, suggesting his belief that the government should avoid 'social interference' at all costs. (Knight 1921a, 194).
4. This embracing of free enterprise and self-interested individualism is similar to other conservative approaches posed in response to Thomas Hobbes' suggestion that individuals were motivated by self-interest, and that a strong government was required to control the barbaric tendencies of individual greed (Hobbes 1651). Adam Smith and followers rejected Hobbes' suggestion of authoritarian control, however, concluding that the free market, with adequate *guidance* from the state, would accomplish the task (see Davidson and Davidson 1988).
5. Followers of Keynes, especially Paul Samuelson (1947), Alvin Hansen (1947, 1949), and Abba Lerner (1949) further articulated his theory, developing fiscal policy recommendations often attributed to Keynes himself. Robinson's reference to the efforts of these and other individual to base principles of macroeconomics upon neoclassical principles of microeconomics as 'Bastard Keynesians' is an indication of her opinion of the accuracy of their interpretation.
6. The influence of Edmund Burke upon Keynes' political thought is evident in Keynes' 'loathing of the bourgeois calculating spirit, a profound contempt for abstract theorizing, a love of county and of civilized sensibilities' (Helburn 1991, 30).

7. Conclusion

The conflicts of interest which give rise to social economic problems relate either to the terms of cooperation or to the rights of individuals to the possession and free use of resources. These two issues make up the general problem of economic ethics.
Frank H. Knight (1945)

It may well be that the classical theory represents the way in which we should like our Economy to behave. But to assume that it actually does so is to assume our difficulties away.
John M. Keynes (1936)

A NEW PARADIGM?

Keynes and Knight both developed an economic analysis that placed uncertainty at the very heart of their work. Each of them recognized that the real world was not one of known outcomes and easily predictable events. Rather, the uncertainty inherent in the real world forced individuals to act in sometimes less than rational ways as a result. Despite the generally accepted notion among orthodox economists that uncertainty poses no real problem for a rational decision-maker, Knight and Keynes believed that this was not necessarily the case.

Classical economists contended that the existence of involuntary unemployment was only a short-run phenomenon that, utilizing a *laissez-faire* policy, would be self-correcting. In fact, their postulate in which demand is created through the process of production itself was perceived as a virtual guarantee that the general condition of full employment would be assured. However, the observation of persistent unemployment in both England and the United States during the early part of the twentieth century created room to doubt the established tenets of classical theory. So, as a result of what Kuhn would call the normal science of continued research and inquiry grew the roots of a new paradigm. To be sure, the old classical paradigm was not abandoned. In fact, it is staunchly adhered to by the majority of those working within the economics profession today. But a period of transition had begun.

In Kuhn's model of scientific revolution, the period of transition between one paradigm and the next is marked by a time in which 'there will be a large but never complete overlap between the problems that can be solved by the old and by the new paradigm' (Kuhn 1962, 85). He went on to suggest that, once the transition from one paradigm to the next is achieved, 'the profession will have changed its view of the field, its methods, and its goals' (Kuhn 1962, 85). Once this transition has occurred, the revolution is complete.

While Kuhn tended to suggest that only one paradigm would ultimately survive this revolutionary process (Kuhn 1962, 19), it is clear that this is far from true in the field of economics. Today, the economics profession is populated by a variety of schools of thought (paradigms) ranging from neoclassicals, who espouse a return to *laissez-faire*, to the so-called Radicals, who contend that the economy is heading toward a great crisis unless there is significant state intervention.

Nonetheless, Keynes' intention was to facilitate the revolution from classical economics to a new economics for a modern world – a new paradigm. With the publication of his *General Theory* over 60 years ago, Keynes attempted to bring into being a scientific revolution in economics, but this revolution has gone largely unrecognized because the orthodox schools of economic theory have failed to liberate themselves of classical axioms. In the years following the publication of the *General Theory*, the field of economics has been littered with diverging views and opinions. In fact, it is readily apparent that many followers of Keynes, some of whom labor under the label of Keynesianism (both old and new), are still reluctant to let go of some of the fundamental tenets of classical economics. Their view is essentially that the system of classical economics is, in fact, the 'general theory' and that the unusual (and special) case of unemployment and under-consumption occurs only because of some short-run imperfection within the market (Davidson, 1994, 10).

While Knight was perhaps less aggressive than Keynes in his criticism of classical (and neoclassical) economic theory, he was still an advocate for change. Even though Knight himself came to accept certain theoretical tenets of classical economics as useful in society's attempt to improve its economic condition, he nonetheless recognized that there were obvious limitations to this general applicability. In particular, he recognized that the existence of uncertainty, combined with certain irrational aspects of human nature, made it problematic to assume that all individuals could make decisions of equal quality and optimal outcome. An unequal and potentially unfair distribution of income could be, and often was, the ultimate outcome of such a system.

Still, Knight was unable to cast aside his overall acceptance of classical economic precepts as a practical choice to be used by society in its quest to improve its economic well being. Therefore Knight, despite his criticism of certain aspects of orthodox economic theory and its frequently unfair results, was unable or unwilling to contribute toward any sort of Kuhnian paradigm shift in the science of economics.

Further preventing the complete transition to a new paradigm is the fact that the 'established' schools of economic thought are self-perpetuating. Beginning in the earliest of undergraduate economics courses and continuing throughout the majority of Ph.D. level programs, the prevailing orthodox ways of thinking are the only ones widely recognized as legitimate. From the elementary basics of microeconomic theory through the advanced mathematical techniques of graduate school, students are exposed and their attention limited to the tenets of neoclassical and new-Keynesian theory. It has been noted that a graduate degree in economics is more an exercise in mathematical trickery than an advanced study of economic theory and policy. Lavoie has fittingly observed that ' ... students of economics must [demonstrate] their ability to comprehend or memorize the most futile of newest neoclassical theoretical developments ... what becomes important ... is not so much the knowledge of the economy or of the overall economic literature, as the ability to learn mathematical techniques of constrained optimization, a panacea linked to the neoclassical presupposition of universal scarcity' (Lavoie, 1992, 15).

Nonetheless, these new-Keynesians continue to profess that their interpretation of Keynes' work does indeed represent a new paradigm. A paradigm shift, as Kuhn describes it is, however, not represented in their work. For example, new-Keynesians cling to the notion of general equilibrium and market-clearing, except in the event of 'sticky' wages and prices which cause inflexibility in the downward direction. While the work of these so-called Keynesians differs from that of the classical economists in that it provides for periods of less than full employment, it merely represents an articulation of classical economics in that the underlying assumptions remain unchanged.

DIVERGENT PERSPECTIVES/COMMON CONCERN

As the end of this investigation into the role of uncertainty in the economic theories of Frank Knight and John Keynes is reached, the divergence of their attitudes toward *laissez-faire* in general, and classical economic theory in particular, has become more clearly understood. To facilitate this understanding, a review of specific influences upon their 'ethics' has been conducted. Their respective understandings and use of probability and uncertainty have been investigated. Likewise, the role and purpose played by economic theory in the lives of individuals and society has been surveyed and the contrasting policy recommendations of Knight and Keynes have been considered. Table 7.2 summarizes the most important points discussed during the course of this study.

The study has led to a reinforcement of the view that both Knight and Keynes sought to preserve the benefits of efficiency and personal freedoms brought about by a free-market economy and that both economists observed potential weaknesses within the widely-accepted, existing economic orthodoxy. Keynes' work was an economics of macro theory, seeking to increase the prosperity of society, by recognizing the fallacy of applying 'the celebrated *optimism* of traditional economic theory' (Keynes 1936, 33) to the real world. Knight deplored the substantial inequities of income and wealth distribution brought about as the result of a system of free markets made up of individuals seeking out their own personal self-interest but possessing insufficient wisdom and intelligence to recognize the costs to society brought about by their self-interested actions.

Keynes observed that classical economic theory should best be ' ... regarded as a theory of distribution in conditions of full employment' (Keynes 1936, 16). This condition, however, is infrequent and occurs only as the result of a random coincidence of equilibrium between supply and demand. The contemporary economic problems of poverty and unemployment observed by Keynes were, in his opinion, the result of economists becoming misled by classical theory and ' ... having left this world for the cultivation of their gardens, teach that all is for the best in the best of all possible worlds provided we will let well alone ... '. They have, according to Keynes, ' ... neglected to take account of the drag on prosperity which can be exercised by an insufficiency of effective demand' (Keynes 1936, 33). The fundamental reason for insufficient effective demand has been established to be the presence of uncertainty within a non-ergodic world.

The tendency for economic agents to respond to such uncertainty by exhibiting a preference for increasing liquidity in the form of holding cash balances results in effective demand too low to satisfy the expectations of businesses. The result is a downward spiral of economic activity leading to high levels of involuntary unemployment.

The recommendations proposed by Keynes were offered not as a replacement for a free-market economy, but as a hopeful attempt to correct the inherent problems within such a system. Keynes' proposals to 'socialize investment', to purposefully manage the rate of interest and to enable the central bank to influence the level of investment, combined with his call for

Table 7.1 Uncertainty and its impact upon the economic theories of Knight and Keynes

	Frank H. Knight	John M. Keynes
Ethical influences	Diverse educational background of philosophy, history, languages, and sciences. Early education occurred at religious, evangelical institutions, latter years spent in more critical, intellectual environment of Cornell University. Significant influences: Conservative, religious family Bergson James	Cambridge intellectualism with emphases on logic, science, and rational thinking. Significant influences: Born into an intellectual, affluent family Marshall Burke Moore
Contemporary social views and environmental influences	American frontier expansion with vast expanses of resources by the blessing of God. Rapid expansion of evangelical religion in two forms – the church and the nation. Individualistic religion of economic and social reward by the hand of God.	Era of enlightened thinking. Inherent goodness of man as a moral and ethical construct. Conflict between theology and science. Intuitionism and utilitarianism.
View of external reality	Predetermined, immutable, ergodic	Unknowable, transmutable, non-ergodic
Observation of the real world	'The reality is not an ideal situation … the present task is to show some of the reasons why – with the facts of nature, man, and society what they are – the framework of free enterprise does not at all imply an ideal social order' (Knight 1960, 97).	Society plagued with two significant problems: to 'provide for full employment and its arbitrary and inequitable distribution of wealth and incomes' (Keynes 1936, 372).

Table 7.1 (con'd)

	Frank H. Knight	**John M. Keynes**
Conception of uncertainty	Situations requiring decisions to be made based upon non-quantifiable factors (as opposed to *risk*). Based upon an ergodic system with epistemological uncertainty.	Situation in which there is no basis upon which to perform any sort of probability analysis. Based upon a non-ergodic system with ontological uncertainty.
Impact of uncertainty upon economic system	Creation of profit, formation of monopoly power, and growing inequities in income and wealth distribution.	Brings about the existence of liquidity preference and the holding of cash balances leading to insufficient effective demand.
Purpose of economics	To explain what does happen and to provide guidance for bringing about what is thought desirable or what ought to happen.	To serve as a tool in reaching a higher level of economic well-being.
Recommendations	Limited, negative role for government to provide and enforce a system of rules and regulations as well as educational reform.	Positive role for government to enact policies to affect the propensities to consume and invest, increasing effective demand.
Vision of the future	A world in which man may pursue his 'chief interest which is to find life interesting'. (Knight 1921a, 369).	A day in which 'the economic problem will take the back seat where it belongs' and humankind will dwell upon 'the problems of life and of human relations, of creation and behaviour and religion' (Keynes 1931, vii).

government spending programs, are directed, not toward the elimination of freedoms, but in the hope of preserving them. Keynes sought purposeful, human intervention in controlling the future progress of society, believing that mankind possessed the requisite skill and intelligence to positively affect the future.

At the heart of his call for action was Keynes' view that, while imperfect, the tools of quantitative analysis could be applied in such a way that the uncertainty of the future could be made *less* threatening to those individuals attempting to make rational decisions. An early observation by Keynes was that ' ... the importance of probability can only be derived from the judgement that it is *rational* to be guided by it in action; and a practical dependence on it can only be justified by a judgement that in action we *ought* to act to take some account of it. It is for this reason that probability is to us the "guide of life," ... ' (Keynes 1921, 323).

Nonetheless, due to the existence of a non-ergodic external reality, Keynes knew of the inherent weaknesses present in any attempt to rely upon probability analysis to predict the future with certainty. He said ' ... it has been pointed out already that no knowledge of probabilities, less in degree than certainty, helps us to know what conclusions are true ... probability begins and ends with probability ... the proposition that a course of action guided by the most probable considerations will generally lead to success, is not certainly true and has nothing to recommend it but its probability' (Keynes 1921, 322). Keynes noted, however, that the confidence possessed by individuals in their own ability to predict the future affects their ability to make rational decisions. It was Keynes' belief that ' ... partly on reasonable and partly on instinctive grounds, our desire to hold Money as a store of wealth is a barometer of the degree of our distrust of our own calculations and conventions concerning the future' (Keynes 1937a, 14). Regardless of Keynes' suggestion early in his life that the use of probability analysis may at times be useful in guiding decision making, he clearly comes to believe that 'most ... of our decisions ... can only be taken as a result of animal spirits ... not as the outcome of a weighted average of quantitative benefits multiplied by quantitative probabilities' (Keynes 1936, 161).

Knight's concern, on the other hand, was less in the ability of a free market system to operate unimpeded by human action and more in his lack of faith in the ability of individuals to maximize the benefits of such a system. Knight struggled with how to reconcile the benefits of a free-market economy characterized by individualistic motives with the ethical costs inherent in such a system. Underlying the orthodox, classical theory were assumptions of rational economic agents, incorporating complete knowledge of past, present, and future events, into a calculation intended to arrive at utility-maximizing decisions. Unlike Keynes, Knight regarded the real world as one that is ergodic, possessing a predictable future based upon the past, as long as one possesses the requisite intellect and rationality to discern it. Uncertainty remains only in those cases of such a unique character that they remain outside the scope of probability analysis. This knowledge led Knight to understand the acceptance of utilitarian ethics by many economists, while providing him a basis for disagreement as well.

According to Knight, the admirers of utility theory did so because it provided the social science of economics with the same sort of mathematical precision that had previously been applied to the natural sciences. Knight observed that 'to its admirers it comes near to being the fulfillment of the eighteenth-century craving for a principle which would do for human conduct and society what Newton's mechanics had done for the solar system' (Knight 1935, 158). Knight believed that the 'simplicity and order' characterized by the application of mathematical functions and 'infinitesimal calculus' to the problems of everyday living attracted many followers to utility theory.

Furthermore, utility theory reinforced for many the 'eighteenth-century cravings, it claims to furnish a guide for social policy; it can be harnessed to the very practical purpose of proving that if only the state will limit itself to the negative function of defence against violence and predation and leave men free to pursue their own interests, individual self-seeking directed by market competition will bring about a simultaneous maximum of want-satisfaction for all concerned ... ' (Knight 1935, 159). Echoing Adam Smith's call for *laissez-faire*, utility theory provided the articulators of classical economic theory with the mathematical precision they needed to support their call for competitive, free markets.

Critics of utility theory, nonetheless, maintained that the application of such techniques to problems of society were unworkable and unrealistic. Knight recognized this fact when he conceded that 'in the more rigorous versions of the theory ... there is an element of paradox and unrealism' and 'under no real circumstances can the behaving subject himself, not to mention any outside observer, ever know even afterward whether or not he actually performed in such a way as to realize maximum possible total satisfaction ... ' (Knight 1935, 159–60). Despite its popularity, Knight therefore believed that such a theory fell short of providing the society of the real world with a totally appropriate analytical system.

As has been established, Knight nonetheless regarded the application of neo-classical theory to economic problems as *useful* in man's effort to improve his ability to make good economic decisions. Specifically, in recognizing that society is ever-changing and progressing through time, Knight incorporated the concept of uncertainty into his model. The existence of *true uncertainty*, as distinguished from probabilistic *risk* reveals the existence of an unquantifiable component inherent in the imperfectly competitive markets of the real world. Still, Knight came to regard *laissez-faire* as the best form of social organization in which the economic game of life could be played. Knight reached this conclusion because such a system, supported by rules enforced by a democratic government, allowed individuals to pursue their own interests, while maintaining social order, with profit the reward for dealing most successfully with the obstacle of uncertainty.

Knight never wavered from his view that the government should limit its role in economic affairs. Beyond the provision of a legal framework of rules, including the clear assignment of property rights and contract enforcement, and the regulating of monopoly power (gained inappropriately),[1] Knight left little room for the government to exert influence. Of all the roles for government to play, however, education remained high on Knight's list of activities in which it could play a productive role. Late in Knight's career, he continued to call for the education of society. In fact, Knight regarded education as the *primary* role for the State to play in economic matters. Knight remarked that 'with respect to political action in the economic sphere, the main task of society, at the present juncture, is *education*, but of the will more than the intellect; it is to develop a more critical attitude' (Knight 1960, 14).

Likewise, Knight never strayed from his consideration of uncertainty as the locus of his economic thinking. He regarded 'the ultimate difficulty with the free economy [to be] that everybody needs to know what everybody else is going to do before he can decide intelligently what he will do' (Knight 1960, 104). Profit, according to Knight, is awarded to those most able to accurately anticipate and plan for the ultimate outcome of an uncertain future. Knight believed that individual profit motives might force the development of monopoly or collusion to solve this problem of uncertainty. Thus Knight's call for political action to regulate and control such potential activity, maintaining an orderly system of competitive markets. But 'the problem is to find the best compromise between freedom and order — how much to leave to individual free choice and voluntary agreement versus what limits to set by enforced general rules' (Knight 1960, 104).

Despite the placement of uncertainty at the heart of their economic thinking, both Knight and Keynes viewed the role of uncertainty from different perspectives. These perspectives are derived from significant, formative influences upon their thinking that led to dramatically different worldviews. Keynes developed the view that the world is characterized by an uncertain future that remains unknowable despite the development and application of advanced statistical techniques. Nevertheless, he still believed that mankind possesses the ability to exert influence upon such a world, having a positive affect upon its future. Knight, on the other hand, concluded that the world is, for the most part, characterized by ergodicity, with the future essentially being like the past. Knight lacked the confidence of Keynes, however, believing mankind to be incapable of effectively dealing with uncertainty because of 'romantic thinking' rather than rationality; the forces of the free market should therefore be allowed to function uninhibited by human action as far as possible.

Specifically, the Cambridge intellectualism in which Keynes was born fostered in him a predilection for logic, science, and rational thinking. Keynes recognized that economics was a tool for the modern world to use in solving its economic problem – the problem of 'poverty in the midst of plenty'. This enlightened thinking allowed Keynes to consider individual and collective action positively, enabling society to take an aggressive role in determining the direction of its own future. With purposeful, deliberate action, society can face an uncertain future with confident self-determination.

The conservative, theological world into which Knight was born fostered a different sort of attitude. With Knight spending most of his formative years in the midst of such religiously-dominated conservative thinking, he nonetheless emerged critical and unaccepting of established orthodox thinking, contrary to most of what he had been taught. While accepting the precepts of classical economic theory as the appropriate model for consideration of the workings of perfect competition, he nonetheless stopped short of believing that such a model had practical application in the real world. Knight was especially critical of classical theory because of its omission of uncertainty as an endogenous variable and for its assumption of the rationality of economic man. In Knight's thinking, given the lack of rational, intelligent thinking, the handling of uncertainty becomes especially problematic. The resulting pessimism regarding man's ability to make rational decisions both individually and collectively left Knight no room for positive action on the part of the state. Other than through its place in educational reform, the government's role becomes essentially a negative one, limited to the establishment and enforcement of 'rules of the game' to be followed by individual economic agents.

Despite differences of perspective, a striking element of commonality remains within the work of Knight and Keynes. Both economists, while disagreeing as to the basis and effect of uncertainty upon economic activity nonetheless recognized, perhaps more than any other two economists of the twentieth century, that the existence of uncertainty indeed has a dramatic impact upon individual and collective decision making. Their mutual abhorrence for the inevitable results of unrestrained capitalism, such as involuntary unemployment and growing income and wealth inequities, led each to suggest that economics be used to improve the conditions of society.

While differing in opinion as to the mechanism through which this improvement was to be achieved, both Knight and Keynes remained passionate in their concern for the ultimate welfare and improvement of mankind.

IS THERE STILL ROOM FOR IMPROVEMENT?

The beginning of the twenty-first century is characterized by widespread economic optimism on a global scale. The recent economic problems in Asia and Eastern Europe seem to have moderated. The United States is continuing to experience historic economic growth, combined with low inflation and low unemployment. How much improvement in the economic welfare of mankind is it reasonable to expect? The present policy of the US Federal Reserve indicates that there certainly may be too much of a good thing. Fearing rampant inflation because of recent acceleration in the growth of Gross Domestic Product, the Federal Reserve has recently enacted its sixth consecutive increase in interest rates, with additional increases possible. Apparently, it is acceptable to force some individuals into unemployment so that society may enjoy lower prices. Still, despite encouraging economic statistics, there continues to be a significant portion of the population which is not sharing in this economic fortune. Income inequality continues to be a serious and growing problem. The percentage of the United States population living in poverty is still approximately 13 per cent, while the World Bank has recently estimated that 1.2 billion people worldwide live at consumption levels equal to $1 US per day. With capitalism continuing to emerge as the predominant form of economic organization, it still appears that there remain individuals who have yet to benefit from the gains of a system of free markets. It remains for economists to develop a body of theory that balances the individual liberty of free markets with the social gains of greater central control. This sort of theory must reexamine the fundamental axioms upon which classical economic theory is built and base itself upon an accurate conception of the real world.

Many have noted that the economy of the modern world dramatically differs from that originally incorporated in the theories of Smith, Ricardo, and their followers. Notably, today's economic world is one of uncertainty, not statistical predictability. Furthermore, modern economies are marked by the non-neutrality of money, unlike the classical notion of money merely serving as a medium of exchange. For these reasons, among others, it can be observed that unacceptably high levels of poverty and periods of involuntary unemployment can and do exist. They are, in fact, more often the rule, rather than the exception (Davidson 1994, 17–18). It is for this reason that policy prescriptions based upon faulty foundations are doomed to fail in a world for which the prevailing assumptions no longer apply. Recent improvements in US economic welfare can at least partially be credited to a realization that there is a role for the government to play in economic matters. The remaining challenge is to develop an economy in which all members of society benefit and in which the individual freedoms of a system of free markets are preserved. This will only occur when economists focus upon the ethical ramification of decision making under conditions of uncertainty. This requires an understanding of human behavior that extends beyond the realm of calculus and into the realm of ethics and philosophy, ground that many economists fear to tread.

NOTE

1. Knight considered 'labor unions and restrictionist farm organizations supported by public opinion and political action' to be less desirable than the more commonly criticized business enterprises (Knight 1960, 99).

Bibliography

Allen, C. Leonard and Richard T. Hughes (1988) *Discovering Our Roots: The Ancestry of the Churches of Christ*, Abilene, Texas: Abilene Christian University Press.

Arestis, Philip and Victoria Chick (1992) *Recent Developments in Post-Keynesian Economic*, Aldershot, U.K.: Edward Elgar.

Ayers, C.E. (1936) 'Discussion: The Ethics of Competition,' *Journal of International Ethics*, **46** (1936): 364–70.

Bastiat, Frederic (1850) *The Law* (trans. Dean Russell), Irvington-On-Hudson, New York: The Foundation for Economic Education (1998).

Bateman, Bradley W. (1987) 'Keynes's Changing Conception of Probability,' *Economics and Philosophy*, **3**: 97–120.

__ (1991) 'The Rules of the Road: Keynes's Theoretical Rationale for Public Policy,' in *Keynes and Philosophy*, Aldershot, U.K.: Edward Elgar, 55–68.

Bateman, Bradley W. and John B. Davis. (1991) *Keynes and Philosophy*, Aldershot, U.K.: Edward Elgar.

__ (1996) *Keynes's Uncertain Revolution*, Ann Arbor: University of Michigan Press.

Baudreaux, D.J. and R.G. Holcombe (1989) 'The Knightian and Coasian Theory of the Firm,' *Managerial and Decision Economics*, **10**: 147–54.

Breit, William and Roger Ransom (1971) *The Academic Scribblers*, New York: Holt, Rinehart and Winston.

Brennan, H. Geoffrey and A.M.C. Waterman (1994) *Economics and Religion: Are They Distinct?*, Norwell, MA: Kluwer.

Bronfenbrenner, M. (1962) 'Observations on the "Chicago School(s)",' *Journal of Political Economy*, **70**: 72–75.

Brue, Stanley (1963) *The Evolution of Economic Thought*, New York: Harcourt Brace (1994).

Buechner, M. Northrop (1976) 'Frank Knight on Capital as the Only Factor of Production,' *Journal of Economic Issues* (Sept.): 598–617.

Carabelli, Anna (1985) 'Keynes on Cause, Chance and Possibility,' in *Keynes' Economics: Methodological Issues* (eds T. Lawson and H. Pesaran), Armonk, NY: Sharpe, 151–80.

__ (1988) *On Keynes's Method,* New York: St. Martin's Press.

__ (1991) 'The Methodology of the Critique of the Classical Theory: Keynes on Organic Interdependence,' in *Keynes and Philosophy* (eds B.W. Bateman and J.B. Davis), Aldershot, U.K.: Edward Elgar, 104–25.

Chick, Victoria (1992) 'The Small Firm Under Uncertainty: A Puzzle of the General Theory,' in *The Philosophy and Economics of J.M. Keynes* (eds B. Gerrard and J. Hillard), Aldershot, U.K.: Edward Elgar, 149–64.

Davidson, Greg and Davidson, Paul (1988) *Economics for a Civilized Society*, New York: W.W. Norton.

Davidson, Paul (1978) *Money and the Real World*, New York: Halsted Press.

__ (1992) 'Uncertainty in Economics,' in *The Philosophy and Economics of J.M. Keynes* (eds B. Gerrard and J. Hillard), Aldershot, U.K.: Edward Elgar, 107–116.

__ (1993) 'Some Misunderstandings on Uncertainty in Modern Classical Economics,' in *Uncertainty in Economic Thought* (ed. Christian Schmidt), Brookfield, Vt. and Aldershot, U.K.: Edward Elgar, 21–37.

__ (1994) *Post-Keynesian Macroeconomic Theory*, Vermont and Aldershot, U.K.: Edward Elgar.

__ (1996) 'Reality and Economic Theory,' *Journal of Post-Keynesian Economics*, **18** (4): 479–508.

__ (1998) 'Post Keynesian Employment Analysis and the Macroeconomics of OECD Unemployment,' *The Economic Journal*, **108** (May): 817–31.

Davis, J.B. (1991a) 'Keynes's Critiques of Moore: Philosophical Foundations of Keynes's Economics,' *Cambridge Journal of Economics*, **15** (1) March: 61–77.

__ (1991b) 'Keynes's View of Economics as a Moral Science,' in *Keynes and Philosophy* (eds B.W. Bateman and J.B. Davis), Aldershot, U.K.: Edward Elgar, 89–103.

Dewey, D. (1986) 'Frank Knight Before Cornell: Some Light on the Dark Years,' Columbia University.

Dewey, John (1908) *Ethics*, New York: Henry Holt and Company.

Dow, Sheila C. (1994) 'The Religious Content of Economics,' in *Economics and Religion: Are They Distinct?* (eds H.G. Brennan and A.M.C. Waterman), Norwell, MA: Kluwer, 193–204.

Durant, Will (1953) *The Story of Philosophy*, New York: Pocket Books (1976).

Dymski, Gary A. (1993) 'Keynesian Uncertainty and Asymmetric Information: Complementary or Contradictory?', *Journal of Post-Keynesian Economics*, **16** (1): 49–54.

Eichner, A.S. and Kregel, J.A. (1975) 'An essay on post-Keynesian theory: a new paradigm in economics,' *Journal of Economic Literature* (Dec. 1975), **13** (4), 1293–1314.

Eisner, R. (1994) 'Keynes is not dead, just drugged and dormant,' *Journal of Post-Keynesian Economics* (Winter 1994–95), **17** (2), 211–29.

Emani, Zohreh (1992) 'History versus Equilibrium: Joan Robinson on Teaching Economics,' *International Journal of Social Economics*, **19** (10/11/12): 83–94.

Emmett, Ross B. (1990) 'The Economist as Philosopher: Frank H. Knight and American Social Science During the Twenties and Early Thirties,' Winnipeg, Manitoba: St. John's College.

__ (1992) 'Frank H. Knight on the Conflict of Values in Economic Life,' *Research in the History of Economic Thought and Methodology*, **9**: 87–103.

__ (1994) 'Frank Knight: Economics versus Religion,' in *Economics and Religion: Are They Distinct?* (eds H.G. Brennan and A.M.C. Waterman), Norwell, MA: Kluwer, 103–120.

__ (1997) 'Reflections on "Breaking Away" Economics as Science and the History of Economics as History of Science,' *Research in the History of Economic Thought and Methodology*, **15**: 221–36.

__ (1999) 'The Economist and the Entrepreneur. Modernist Impulses in Frank H. Knight's *Risk, Uncertainty, and Profit*,' *History of Political Economy*, **31** (1): 29–52.

Fitzgibbons, Athol (1991) 'The Significance of Keynes's Idealism,' in *Keynes and Philosophy* (eds B.W. Bateman and J.B. Davis), Aldershot, U.K.: Edward Elgar, 126–32.

Fogde, Myron J. (1977) *Faith of Our Fathers – The Church Goes West*, Wilmington, NC USA: Consortium.

Foss, Nicolai Juui (1993) 'More on Knight and the Theory of the Firm,' *Managerial and Decision Economics*, **14**: 269–76.

__ (1996) 'The Alternative Theories of Knight and Coase, and the Modern Theory of the Firm,' *Journal of History of Economic Thought*, **18**: 76–95.

Garello, Pierre (1993) 'Uncertainty and Subjectivism: The Role of Uncertainty in the Austrian School,' in *Uncertainty in Economic Thought* (ed. Christian Schmidt), Brookfield, Vt. and Aldershot, U.K.: Edward Elgar, 87–99.

Garner, C. Alan (1983) '"Uncertainty" in Keynes' General Theory: A Comment,' *History of Political Economy*, **15** (1): 83–91.

Gerrard, Bill and John Hillard (1992) *The Philosophy and Economics of J.M. Keynes*, Aldershot, U.K.: Edward Elgar.

Gonce, R.A. (1992) 'Frank H. Knight on Social Control and the Scope and Method of Economics,' Repr. in *Frank Knight (1885–1972), Henry Simons*

(1899–1946), Joseph Schumpeter (1883–1950) Elgar Reference Series, Pioneers in Economics Series (ed. M. Blaug), Vol 37. Brookfield, Vt. and Aldershot, U.K.: Edward Elgar, 22–33.

Greenaway, David, Michael Bleaney, and Ian Stewart (1991) *Companion to Contwmporary Economic Thought*, London: Routledge.

Hagerman, Harald and O.F. Hamouda (1994) *The Legacy of Hicks: His Contribution to Economic Analysis*, London: Routledge.

Hamouda, Omar F. and John N. Smithin (1988) 'Some Remarks on "Uncertainty and Economic Analysis,"' *The Economic Journal* (Jan.): 159–64.

Hands, D. Wade (1997) 'Frank Knight's Pluralism' in *Pluralism in Economics – New Perspectives in History and Methodology* (eds A. Salanti and E. Screpanti), Cheltenham, U.K.: Edward Elgar, 194–206.

Hansen, Alvin (1947) *Economic Policy and Full Employment*, New York: McGraw-Hill.

__ (1949) *Monetary Theory and Fiscal Policy*, New York: McGraw-Hill.

__ (1953) *A Guide to Keynes*, New York: McGraw-Hill.

Heilbroner, Robert (1953) *The Worldly Philosophers*, New York: Simon and Schuster (1980).

Heilbroner, Robert and Milberg, William (1962) *The Making of Economic Society*, New York: Prentice-Hall (1998).

Helburn, Suzanne W. 1991. 'Burke and Keynes,' in *Keynes and Philosophy* (eds B.W. Bateman and J.B. Davis), Aldershot, U.K.: Edward Elgar 30–54.

__ (1992) 'On Keynes's Ethics,' in *Recent Developments in Post-Keynesian Economics* (eds P. Arestis and V. Chick), Aldershot, U.K.: Edward Elgar, 27–46.

Hey, John D. (1983) 'Whither Uncertainty?', *Economic Journal*, March: 130–39.

__ (1991) 'Uncertainty in Economics,' in *Companion to Contemporary Economic Thought* (eds D. Greenaway, M. Bleaney, and I. Stewart), London: Routledge, 252–76.

__ (1994) 'Risk and Uncertainty,' in *The Legacy of Hicks: His Contribution to Economic Analysis* (eds H. Hagemann and O.F. Hamouda), London: Routledge, 187–99.

Hillard, John (1992) 'Keynes, Orthodoxy and Uncertainty,' in *The Philosophy and Economics of J.M. Keynes* (eds B. Gerrard and J. Hillard), Aldershot, U.K.: Edward Elgar, 59–79.

Hobbes, Thomas (1651) *Leviathan*, New York: E.P. Dutton & Co. (1931).

Hoogduin, L. (1987) 'On the Difference Between the Keynesian, Knightian and the "Classical" Analysis of Uncertainty and the Development of a More General Monetary Theory,' *De Economist*, **135** (1): 52–65.

Jensen, Hans E. (1983) 'J.M. Keynes as a Marshallian,' *Journal of Economic Issues*, (March): 67–94.

__ (1994) 'Aspects of J.M. Keynes's Vision and Conceptualized Reality,' in *The State of Interpretation of Keynes*, 167–204.

Kaldor, Nicholas and James Trevithick (1981) 'A Keynesian Perspective on Money,' *Lloyds Bank Review* (Jan.): 101–19.

Kasper, Sherryl (1993) 'Frank Knight's Case for Laissez Faire: The Patrimony of the Social Philosophy of the Chicago School," *History of Political Economy*, **25** (3): 413–33.

Keynes, John M. (1919) *The Economic Consequences of the Peace*, New York: Penguin (1995).

__ (1921) *A Treatise on Probability*, London: McMillan (1962).

__ (1922) *A Revision of the Treaty*, New York: Harcourt, Brace and Co.

__ (1926) 'The End of Laissez-Faire,' in *Small Firms and Economic Growth Volume 1* (ed. J. Zoltan), Cheltenham, U.K.: Edward Elgar (1996).

__ (1930a) Letter from *The Journal of the Royal Statistical Society – Part I*, in *The General Theory and After. Part I: Preparation* (ed. Donald Moggridge), 127–30. Vol. 13 of *The Collected Writings of John Maynard Keynes*, London: The Macmillan Press (1973).

__ (1930b) 'Economic Possibilities for Our Grandchildren,' in *Essays in Persuasion*, 358–73. New York: Harcourt, Brace and Co. (1932).

__ (1931) *Essays in Persuasion*, New York: Harcourt, Brace and Co. (1932).

__ (1934) 'Poverty in Plenty: Is the Economic System Self-Adjusting?', from *The Listener*, Nov. 21. in *The General Theory and After. Part I: Preparation* (ed. Donald Moggridge), 485–92. Vol. 13 of *The Collected Writings of John Maynard Keynes*, London: The Macmillan Press (1973).

__ (1936) *The General Theory of Employment, Interest and Money*, New York: Harcourt, Brace and Co. (1991).

__ (1937a) 'The General Theory of Employment,' from *The Quarterly Journal of Economics*, February. In *The Keynesian Heritage* (ed. G.K. Shaw), 7–21. Aldershot, U.K.: Edward Elgar (1988).

__ (1937b) 'Some Economic Consequences of A Declining Population,' from *The Eugenics Review*, April. In *The General Theory and After. Part II: Defence and Development* (ed. Donald Moggridge), 124–33. Vol. 14 of *The Collected Writings of John Maynard Keynes*, London: The Macmillan Press (1972).

__ (1938a) Letter to Roy Harrod of July 4. In *The General Theory and After. Part II: Defence and Development* (ed. Donald Moggridge), 295–7. Vol. 14 of *The Collected Writings of John Maynard Keynes*, London: The Macmillan Press (1972).

__ (1938b) Letter to Roy Harrod of July 6. In *The General Theory and After. Part II: Defence and Development*, (ed. Donald Moggridge), 299–301.

Vol. 14 of *The Collected Writings of John Maynard Keynes*, London: The Macmillan Press (1972).

__ (1938c) 'My Early Beliefs,' in *Essays in Biography* (ed. Donald Moggridge), 430–50. Vol. 10 of *The Collected Writings of John Maynard Keynes*, London: The Macmillan Press (1972).

Khalil, Elias (1997) 'Chaos Theory versus Heisenberg's Uncertainty: Risk, Uncertainty, and Economic Theory,' *American Economist* (Fall): 27–41.

Knight, Frank H. (1921a) *Risk, Uncertainty, and Profit*, New York: Houghton Mifflin Company (1957).

__ [1921b] (1935) 'Cost of Production and Price Over Long and Short Periods,' in Knight (1935a).

__ [1922] (1935) 'Ethics and the Economic Interpretation,' in Knight (1935a).

__ [1923] (1935) 'The Ethics of Competition,' in Knight (1935a).

__ [1924] (1935) 'Fallacies in the Interpretation of Social Cost,' in Knight (1935a).

__ [1925] (1935) 'Economic Psychology and the Value Problem,' in Knight (1935a).

__ [1928] (1956) 'Historical and Theoretical Issues in the Problem of Modern Capitalism,' in Knight (1956).

__ (1929) 'Freedom as Fact and Criterion,' *International Journal of Ethics* (39) 2: 129–47.

__ [1930] (1935) 'Statics and Dynamics: Some Queries Regarding the Mechanical Analogy in Economics,' in Knight (1935a).

__ (1932) 'The Case for Communism,' drafts for a lecture for the National Student League, November 2, 1932 and the Graduate Club of Economics and Business, November 9, 1932. Box 2, Folders 1–9. Frank Knight Papers, Special Collections, Joseph Regenstein Library, Univ. of Chicago, Chicago.

__ [1934] (1935) 'Economic Theory and Nationalism,' in Knight (1935a).

__ (1935a) *The Ethics of Competition*, New York: Harper and Brothers.

__ (1935b) 'The Ricardian Theory of Production and Distribution,' in Knight (1956).

__ [1936] (1947) 'Pragmatism and Social Action,' in Knight (1947a).

__ [1939] (1947) 'Ethics and Economic Reform,' in Knight (1947a).

__ [1940a] (1947) 'Socialism: The Nature of the Problem,' in Knight (1947a).

__ [1940b] (1956) '"What is Truth" in Economics?', in Knight (1956).

__ [1941a] (1947) 'Religion and Ethics in Modern Civilization,' in Knight (1947a).

__ [1941b] (1947) 'The Meaning of Democracy: Its Politico-Economic Structure and Ideal,' in Knight (1947a).

__ [1941c] (1956) 'Social Science,' in Knight (1956).

__ [1941d] (1956). 'The Business Cycle, Interest, and Money A Methodological Approach,' in Knight (1956).

__ [1942a] (1947) 'Science, Philosophy, and Social Procedure,' in Knight (1947a).

__ [1942b] (1947) 'Fact and Value in Social Science,' in Knight (1947a).

__ [1942c] (1947) 'Some Notes on the Economic Interpretation of History,' in Knight (1947a).

__ [1943] (1956) 'Social Causation,' in Knight (1956).

__ [1944a] (1947) 'Economics, Political Science, and Education,' in Knight (1947a).

__ [1944b] (1947) 'The Rights of Man and Natural Law,' in Knight (1947a).

__ [1944c] (1947) 'Human Nature and World Democracy,' in Knight (1947a).

__ [1944d] (1947) 'Economics, Political Science, and Education,' in Knight (1947a).

__ [1944e] (1947) 'The Planful Act: The Possibilities and Limitations of Collective Rationality,' in Knight (1947a).

__ [1946] (1947) 'The Sickness of Liberal Society,' in Knight (1947a).

__ (1947a) *Freedom and Reform*, New York: Harper and Brothers.

__ [1947b] (1956) 'Salvation by Science: The Gospel According to Professor Lundberg,' in Knight (1956).

__ [1948] (1956) 'Free Society: Its Basic Nature and Problem,' in Knight (1956).

__ (1951a) *The Economic Organization*, New York: Harper and Rowe.

__ [1951b] (1956) 'Economics,' in Knight (1956).

__ [1951c] (1956) 'The Role of Principles in Economics and Politics,' in Knight (1956).

__ (1956) *On the History and Method of Economics*, Chicago: University of Chicago Press.

__ (1960) *Intelligence and Democratic Action*, Cambridge, Massachusetts: Harvard University Press.

__ and Merriam, Thornton W. (1945). *The Economic Order and Religion*, New York: Harper and Brothers.

Kregel, J.A. (1976) 'Economic Methodology in the Face of Uncertainty: The Modelling Methods of Keynes and the Post-Keynesians,' *The Economic Journal* (June): 209–25.

Kuhn, Thomas S. (1962) *The Structure of Scientific Revolutions*, Chicago: University of Chicago Press.

Kyburg, Henry E. Jr. (1961) *Probability and the Logic of Rational Belief*, Middletown, CT: Wesleyan University Press.

Landreth, Harry and David Colander (1994) *History of Economic Thought*, Boston: Houghton Mifflin.

Langlois, Richard N. and Metin M. Cosgel (1993) 'Frank Knight on Risk, Uncertainty, and the Firm: A New Interpretation,' *Economic Inquiry* (July): 456–65.

Lavoie, Marc (1992) *Foundations of Post-Keynesian Economic Analysis*, Aldershot, U.K.: Edward Elgar.

Lawson, Tony (1988) 'Probability and Uncertainty in Economic Analysis,' *Journal of Post Keynesian Economics* (Fall): 38–65.

Lawson, Tony and Hashem Pesaran (1985) *Keynes' Economics: Methodological Issues*, Armonk, NY: Sharpe.

Lerner, Abba (1949) *The Economics of Control*, New York: Macmillan.

Leroy, Stephen R. and Larry D. Singell, Jr. (1987) 'Knight on Risk and Uncertainty,' *Journal of Political Economy* (April): 394–406.

Leuchtenburg, William E. (1958) *The Perils of Prosperity 1914–32*, Chicago: University of Chicago Press.

Levine, David P. (1997) 'Knowing and Acting: On Uncertainty in Economics,' *Review of Political Economy* (January): 5–17.

Makasheva, Nataliia (1993) 'Ethics and the General Economic Theory (The Intellectual Challenge of J.M. Keynes,' *Problems of Economic Transition* (August): 74–94.

Marshall, Alfred (1890) *Principles of Economics, 8th edn*, London: Macmillan (1920).

McKinney, John W. (1977) 'Frank Knight on Uncertainty and Rational Action,' *Southern Economic Journal* (April): 1438–542.

McLoughlin, William G. (1978) *Revivals, Awakenings, and Reform*, Chicago: University of Chicago Press.

Mead, Sidney (1963) *The Lively Experiment: The Shaping of Christianity in America*, New York: Harper & Row.

Mini, Piero V. (1991) *Keynes, Bloomsbury and The General Theory*, New York: St. Martin's Press.

Moore, Basil J. (1983) 'Unpacking the Post-Keynesian Black Box: Bank Lending and the Money Supply,' *Journal of Post Keynesian Economics*, V (4): 537–56.

Moore, G.E. (1903) *Principia Ethica*, Cambridge: Cambridge University Press (1956).

Nash, Stephen John (1998) *Cost, Uncertainty, and Welfare: Frank Knight's Theory of Imperfect Competition*, Aldershot, U.K.: Ashgate.

Netter, Maurice (1993) 'Radical Uncertainty and its Economic Scope According to Knight and According to Keynes,' in *Uncertainty in Economic Thought* (ed. Christian Schmidt), Brookfield, Vt. and Aldershot, U.K.: Edward Elgar, 65–84.

Newbigin, Lesslie, (1995). *Proper Confidence: Faith, Doubt, and Certainty in Christian Discipleship*, Grand Rapids, MI: Wm. B. Eerdmans.

Norman, Alfred L. and David W. Shimer (1994) 'Risk, Uncertainty, and Complexity,' *Journal of Economic Dynamics and Control* (January): 231–49.

O'Donnell, R.M. (1989) *Keynes: Philosophy, Economics and Politics*, New York: St. Martin's Press.

__ (1991) *Keynes as Philosopher-Economist*, New York: St. Martin's.

__ (1991) 'Keynes's Weight of Argument and its Bearing on Rationality and Uncertainty,' in *Keynes and Philosophy* (eds B.W. Bateman and J.B. Davis), Aldershot, U.K.: Edward Elgar, 69–88.

Paley, William (1785) *The Principles of Moral and Political Philosophy*, Boston: Bazin & Elsworth (1932).

Perlman, Mark and Charles R. McCann, Jr. (1993) 'Varieties of Uncertainty,' in *Uncertainty in Economic Thought* (ed. Christian Schmidt), Brookfield, Vt. and Aldershot, U.K.: Edward Elgar, 9-20.

Raines, J. Patrick and Clarence R. Jung, Jr. (1992) 'Schumpeter and Knight on Economic and Political Rationality: A Comparative Restatement,' *The Journal of Socio-Economics*, **21** (2): 109–24.

Runde, Jochen (1992) 'Risk, Uncertainty and Bayesian Decision Theory: A Keynesian View,' in *The Philosophy and Economics of J.M. Keynes* (eds B. Gerrard and J. Hillard), Aldershot, U.K.: Edward Elgar, 197-210.

__ (1994) 'Keynesian Uncertainty and Liquidity Preference,' *Cambridge Journal of Economics*, **18**: 129–44.

Rymes, T.K. (1994) 'Keynes and Knowledge,' in *Economics and Religion: Are They Distinct?* (eds H.G. Brennan and A.M.C. Waterman), Norwell, MA: Kluwer, 139–59.

Salanti, Andrea and Ernesto Screpanti. (1997) *Pluralism in Economics: New Perspectives in History and Methodology*, Cheltenham, U.K.: Edward Elgar.

Samuelson, Paul (1947) *Foundations of Economic Analysis*, New York: McGraw-Hill.

Sawyer, Malcolm (1991) 'Uncertainty in Economics,' in *Companion to Contemporary Economic Thought* (eds H.G. Brennan and A.M.C. Waterman), London: Routledge, 184–206.

Schmidt, Christian (1993) *Uncertainty in Economic Thought*, Brookfield, Vt. and Aldershot, U.K.: Edward Elgar.

__ (1993) 'Introduction: What is Certainty in Economic Thought,' in *Uncertainty in Economic Thought* (ed. Christian Schmidt), Brookfield, Vt. and Aldershot, U.K.: Edward Elgar, 1–6.

__ (1993) 'Risk and Uncertainty: a Knightian Distinctioin Revisited,' in *Uncertainty in Economic Thought* (ed. Christian Schmidt), Brookfield, Vt. and Aldershot, U.K.: Edward Elgar, 65–84.

Schweikhardt, David B. (1988) 'The Role of Values in Economic Theory and Policy: A Comparison of Frank Knight and John Commons,' *Journal of Economic Issues* (June): 407–14.

Schweitzer, Arthur (1975) 'Frank Knight's Social Economics,' *History of Political Economy*, 7 (3): 279–92.

Shackle, G.L.S. (1973) *Keynesian Keleidics*, Edinburgh: Edinburgh University Press (1974).

Shionoya, Yuichi (1991) 'Sidgwick, Moore and Keynes: A Philosophical Analysis of Keynes's "My Early Beliefs",' in *Keynes and Philosophy* (eds B.W. Bateman and J.B. Davis), Aldershot, U.K.: Edward Elgar, 6–29.

Sidgwick, Henry (1874) *The Methods of Ethics*, Chicago: University of Chicago Press (1962).

Skidelsky, Robert (1986) *John Maynard Keynes: Hopes Betrayed. 1883–1920*, New York: Viking Penguin.

__ (1992) *John Maynard Keynes: The Economist as Savior. 1920–1937*, New York: The Penguin Press.

Smith, Adam (1759) *The Theory of Moral Sentiments*, Indianapolis: Liberty Classics (1976).

__ (1776) *The Nature and Causes of the Wealth of Nations: A Selected Edition*, New York: Oxford University Press (1993).

Stigler, George (1988) *Memoirs of an Unregulated Economist*, New York: Basic Books.

Stohs, Mark (1980) '"Uncertainty" in Keynes' General Theory,' *History of Political Economy*, 12 (3): 372–82.

__ (1983) '"Uncertainty" in Keynes' General Theory: A Rejoinder,' *History of Political Economy*, 15 (1): 87–91.

Tawney, R.H. (1962) *Religion and the Rise of Capitalism*, Gloucester, Mass: Peter Smith.

Valiente, Wilfredo Santiago (1980) 'Is Frank Knight the Victor in the Controversy Between the Two Cambridges?', *History of Political Economy*, 12 (1): 41–64.

Van Der Feltz, W.J. and L.H. Hoogduin (1988) 'Rational Formation of Expectations: Keynesian Uncertainty and Davidson's (Non) Ergodicity-Criterium,' *Metroeconomica*, 39 (2): 105–19.

Veblen, T. (1899) *The Theory of The Leisure Class*, Reprint. New York: New American Library (1963).

Vini, Piero V. (1991) *Keynes, Bloomsbury and The General Theory*, New York: St. Martin's Press.

Weber, M. (1904) *The Protestant Ethic and the Spirit of Capitalism*, Reprint. New York: Charles Scribner's Sons (1958).

Weintraub, E. Roy (1975) '"Uncertainty" and the Keynesian Revolution,' *History of Political Economy*, **7** (4): 530–48.

Index